The Road to Stalingrad

By the Editors of Time-Life Books

Alexandria, Virginia

TIME
LIFE ®

Time-Life Books Inc.
is a wholly owned subsidiary of
The Time Inc. Book Company
Time-Life Books Inc.

Managing Editor: Thomas H. Flaherty
Director of Editorial Resources:
Elise D. Ritter-Clough
Director of Photography and Research:
John Conrad Weiser
Editorial Board: Dale M. Brown, Roberta Conlan,
Laura Foreman, Lee Hassig, Jim Hicks, Blaine
Marshall, Rita Thievon Mullin, Henry Woodhead

PUBLISHER: Joseph J. Ward

Editorial Director: Russell B. Adams, Jr.
Marketing Director: Anne C. Everhart
Director of Design: Louis Klein
Production Manager: Marlene Zack
Supervisor of Quality Control: James King

Editorial Operations
Production: Celia Beattie
Library: Louise D. Forstall
Computer Composition: Deborah G. Tait
(Manager), Monika D. Thayer,
Janet Barnes Syring, Lillian Daniels

The Third Reich

SERIES EDITOR: Henry Woodhead
Series Administrator: Jane Edwin
Art Director: Raymond Ripper
Picture Editor: Jane Jordan
Editorial Staff for *The Road to Stalingrad:*
Text Editor: John Newton
Associate Editors/Research: Kirk Denkler
(principal), Karen Monks, Trudy Pearson
Assistant Editor/Research: Maggie Debelius
(principal)
Assistant Art Director: Lorraine D. Rivard
Writers: Charles J. Hagner, Stephanie A. Lewis
Copy Coordinator: Anne Farr
Picture Coordinator: Jennifer Iker
Editorial Assistant: Jayne A. L. Dover

Special Contributors: Ronald H. Bailey,
George Daniels, Donald Dale Jackson, Brian C.
Pohanka, David S. Thomson (text); Martha Lee
Beckington (research); Alan Schager (administra-
tion); Roy Nanovic (index)

Correspondents: Elisabeth Kraemer-Singh
(Bonn), Christine Hinze (London), Christina
Lieberman (New York), Maria Vincenza Aloisi
(Paris), Ann Natanson (Rome). Valuable
assistance was also provided by: Judy Aspinall
(London); Sasha Isachenko (Moscow); Ann Wise
(Rome); Elizabeth Brown, Katheryn White.

Other Publications:

TIME-LIFE LIBRARY OF CURIOUS AND UNUSUAL FACTS
AMERICAN COUNTRY
VOYAGE THROUGH THE UNIVERSE
THE TIME-LIFE GARDENER'S GUIDE
MYSTERIES OF THE UNKNOWN
TIME FRAME
FIX IT YOURSELF
FITNESS, HEALTH & NUTRITION
SUCCESSFUL PARENTING
HEALTHY HOME COOKING
UNDERSTANDING COMPUTERS
LIBRARY OF NATIONS
THE ENCHANTED WORLD
THE KODAK LIBRARY OF CREATIVE PHOTOGRAPHY
GREAT MEALS IN MINUTES
THE CIVIL WAR
PLANET EARTH
COLLECTOR'S LIBRARY OF THE CIVIL WAR
THE EPIC OF FLIGHT
THE GOOD COOK
WORLD WAR II
HOME REPAIR AND IMPROVEMENT
THE OLD WEST

For information on and a full description of any
of the Time-Life Books series listed above, please
call 1-800-621-7026 or write:
Reader Information
Time-Life Customer Service
P.O. Box C-32068
Richmond, Virginia 23261-2068

The Cover: In October 1942, German troops make
their way through a field of rubble past the Red
Barricade, a wrecked ordnance plant on the industrial north side of Stalingrad. Resurgent Soviet
troops surrounded the city in November and destroyed the German Sixth Army, opening the way
for further counterattacks that foiled Hitler's bid to
seize the oil fields of the Caucasus and threatened
to annihilate the Wehrmacht's forces in southern
Russia.

This volume is one of a series that chronicles
the rise and eventual fall of Nazi Germany. Other
books in the series include:
The SS
Fists of Steel
Storming to Power
The New Order
The Reach for Empire
Lightning War
Wolf Packs
Conquest of the Balkans
Afrikakorps
The Center of the Web
Barbarossa
War on the High Seas
The Twisted Dream

First printing. Printed in U.S.A.

Published simultaneously in Canada.
School and library distribution by Silver Burdett
Company, Morristown, New Jersey 07960.

TIME-LIFE is a trademark of Time Warner Inc.
U.S.A.

**Library of Congress Cataloging in
Publication Data**
The Road to Stalingrad / by the editors of
Time-Life Books.
   p.   cm. — (The Third Reich)
   Includes bibliographical references and index.
   ISBN 0-8094-8150-2
   ISBN 0-8094-8151-0 (lib. bdg.)
   1. World War, 1939-1945—Campaigns—Russian
S.F.S.R.
2. Stalingrad, Battle of, 1942-1943.
I. Time-Life Books. II. Series.
D764.R563 1990   940.54'21785—dc20   90-38954

General Consultants

Col. John R. Elting, USA (Ret.), former associate professor at West Point, has written
or edited some twenty books, including
Swords around a Throne, *The Superstrate-
gists*, and *American Army Life*, as well as
Battles for Scandinavia in the Time-Life
Books World War II series. He was chief con-
sultant to the Time-Life series The Civil War.

Charles V. P. von Luttichau is an associate
at the U.S. Army Center of Military History in
Washington, D.C., and coauthor of *Command Decision* and *Great Battles*. From 1937
to 1945, he served in the German air force
and taught at the Air Force Academy in Berlin. After the war, he emigrated to the United
States and was a historian in the Office of the
Chief of Military History, Department of the
Army, from 1951 to 1986, when he retired.

Contents

Adolf Hitler and a group of his generals discuss *Fall Blau*—"Case Blue"—the renewal of the offensive against the Soviet Union, at Army Group South's headquarters in the Ukraine on June 1, 1942. While his adjutant, Rudolf Schmundt *(far left)*, talks with Maximilian von Weichs, commander of the Second Army, Hitler makes a point with Hans von Salmuth, soon to take over temporary command of the Fourth Army. Friedrich Paulus, commander of the Sixth Army *(facing camera)*, is chatting with Wilhelm Keitel, chief of the armed forces high command.

A number of Hitler's commanders harbored doubts about operation Blau, an ambitious scheme to drive deep into the Caucasus, seize vital oil fields, and encircle and destroy the vast numbers of Russian troops who would doubtless rise to the defense.

A Grand Scheme for Victory in the East

The spring season for which the exhausted German army had so desperately yearned was only a week old when General Franz Halder rode in his staff car through the towering beech forests near Rastenburg in East Prussia. It was March 28, 1942, and the professorial-looking chief of the army high command was en route to an important conference at Wolfsschanze (Wolf's Lair), the compound of camouflaged concrete bunkers and wooden huts—a cross between a concentration camp and a monastery, one general called it—from which Adolf Hitler directed the war.

Gusty winds lashed the trees, but less furiously now that they carried the new season's promise of warmth. To the east, in the Soviet Union, spring was already thawing the frozen battlefront that stretched for more than 1,500 miles from the Barents Sea in the north to the Black Sea in the south. With the thaw came quagmires of mud, restricting movement by either side. And with the forced truce came speculation in the German ranks about when and where the high command would renew the offensive.

Halder was all too aware that the winter's losses made it foolish to even contemplate the kind of broad attack that had characterized Operation Barbarossa, the initial invasion of Russia launched the previous June. This year, the Germans would have to focus on one sector. Hitler already had confided to Halder where he intended to strike once the roads had dried. Not in the north, where Leningrad was still holding out against the German siege, despite the death by disease and starvation of almost a million citizens. Not in the center, where the surprise Russian counteroffensive, combined with sub-zero temperatures, had turned back German spearheads less than twenty miles from Moscow the previous December.

Instead, in a far more audacious stroke, Hitler wanted Army Group South to stab southeastward through the Ukraine into the Caucasus. This resource-rich region, between the Black and Caspian seas, accounted for 70 percent of Soviet oil production. Once the Wehrmacht had seized the oil fields, cutting off supplies to Russia and enhancing Germany's own precarious reserves, Hitler planned to plunge farther southward. His columns would cross into Iran and deprive the Soviet Union of a principal

During Hitler's push for the Caucasus in the early summer of 1942, an advance panzer unit transforms a sleepy Ukrainian village into an armed camp bristling with tanks, half-tracks, and staff vehicles. At center, officers discuss tactics near a command car while in the foreground tank crewmen await their orders.

supply line for shipments of supplies from the United States. Then the German forces would link up with General Erwin Rommel's Afrikakorps, which meanwhile would have slashed through the British armies defending Egypt and seized the petroleum wealth of the Arabian Peninsula.

Halder had doubts about the grandiose plan. In the nine months since invading Russia, Germany had lost nearly 1.1 million men killed, wounded, or missing, plus a half-million to illness or frostbite. Most of the infantry divisions were operating with only 50 percent of full manpower and such inadequate transport that some reconnaissance battalions still traveled on bicycles. Of the 74,000 personnel carriers and other vehicles lost during the terrible winter, a mere 10 percent had been replaced; similarly, scarcely more than one-tenth of the 180,000 dead pack animals had been replaced. Until the army could regain its strength, Halder favored a limited offensive, preferably against the high command's favorite target—Moscow.

But when Halder arrived at Wolfsschanze that windy March day, he kept his doubts conspicuously in check. Although one witness wrote later that Halder's "discomfort could be felt almost physically" during the three-hour session, the chief of the army high command presented without objections an operational plan that echoed the Führer's own intentions. The cautious general, who formerly had spoken frankly to the Führer on such matters as enemy manpower and armaments, now seldom bothered him with unpleasant facts. "Any logical discussion was out of the question," Halder said of Hitler after the war. "He would foam at the mouth, threaten me with his fists, and scream at the top of his lungs."

After the meeting, Hitler turned over the plan to the staff of his armed forces high command for refinement. The Führer had meddled in tactical and operational matters from the beginning of the Russian campaign. And since taking over as commander in chief of the army in December 1941, he had persuaded himself that only his steady refusal to bow to his generals' calls for retreat had brought the army safely through the winter. Although visitors to Wolfsschanze reported him gray and drawn, Hitler insisted on intervening in all phases of the fighting, down to the movements of units as small as infantry battalions. Thus, no one was surprised when he expressed dissatisfaction with the revision of the plan a week after the conference with Halder. The new version, Hitler felt, granted too much freedom to the commanders in the field. "I will deal with the matter myself," he announced, and then began rewriting large sections of it.

On April 5, 1942, he issued Führer Directive no. 41, detailing the objectives for his eastern armies during the coming months. The major offensive in the south was now code-named *Blau* (Blue), replacing the high command's working title, Siegfried; the failure of Barbarossa to produce a quick

In early May of 1942, three German army groups stood astride a convoluted front that zigzagged 1,500 miles from the Gulf of Finland in the north to the Black Sea in the south. Rejecting recommendations to renew the push on Moscow, Hitler set his sights on the oil fields of the Caucasus. But first he would have to annihilate the Red Army forces between the Donets River and the great bend in the Don River west of Stalingrad. His plan to achieve this, code-named *Blau* (Blue), called for a series of envelopments by Army Group South. While the troops of Army Groups Center and North stabilized their sectors by wiping out pockets of enemy troops and partisans behind the lines, Army Group South, in preparation for the main assault, would drive the Soviets from the Kerch Peninsula in the eastern Crimea, renew the siege of Sevastopol, and eliminate the Soviet salient at Izyum. Operation Blau could then commence. The northern wing of Army Group South would execute a pincers movement aimed at entrapping Soviet forces west of Voronezh. Then the two arms of the northern wing would unite, drive southeast to Millerovo, and link up with troops pushing eastward from the Kharkov area. These forces would head east and join with Army Group South's southern wing in a third encirclement between the lower Donets and Stalingrad. With the northern flank secure, a three-pronged drive into the Caucasus could begin.

Bold Plans for the Southern Flank

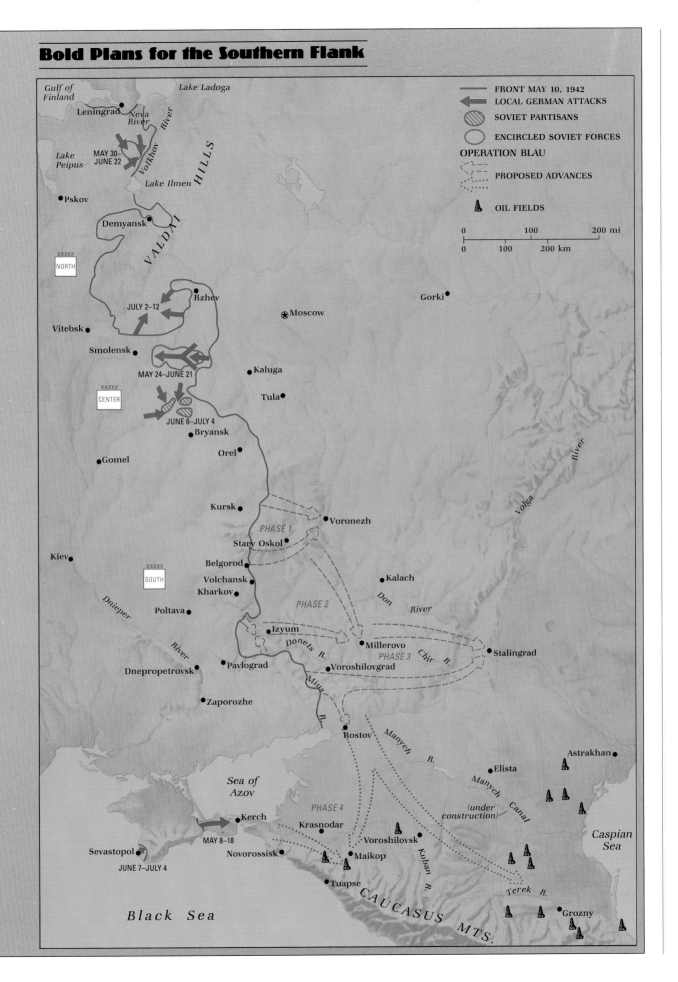

FRONT MAY 10, 1942
LOCAL GERMAN ATTACKS
SOVIET PARTISANS
ENCIRCLED SOVIET FORCES
OPERATION BLAU
PROPOSED ADVANCES
OIL FIELDS

0   100   200 mi
0   100   200 km

Gulf of Finland
Lake Ladoga
Leningrad
Neva River
Volkhov River
Lake Peipus
MAY 30–JUNE 22
Lake Ilmen
Pskov
Demyansk
VALDAI HILLS
XXXXX NORTH
JULY 2–12
Rzhev
Gorki
Moscow
Vitebsk
Smolensk
Kaluga
MAY 24–JUNE 21
Tula
XXXXX CENTER
JUNE 6–JULY 4
Bryansk
Orel
Gomel
Kursk
Voronezh
PHASE 1
Stary Oskol
Volga River
Kiev
Belgorod
XXXXX SOUTH
Volchansk
Kalach
Kharkov
Don River
PHASE 2
Poltava
Izyum
Donets R.
Millerovo
Chir R.
Stalingrad
PHASE 3
Dnepropetrovsk
Pavlograd
Voroshilovgrad
Dnieper River
Zaporozhe
Mius R.
Rostov
Manych R.
Astrakhan
Elista
Manych Canal
Sea of Azov
(under construction)
PHASE 4
Caspian Sea
Kerch
Krasnodar
MAY 8–18
Voroshilovsk
Sevastopol
Novorossisk
Maikop
Kuban R.
JUNE 7–JULY 4
Tuapse
Terek R.
Grozny
CAUCASUS MTS.
Black Sea

victory had apparently soured Hitler on operations named after Teutonic heroes. As redrafted by the Führer, the directive laid out the tactics of Blau in excruciating detail while blurring the strategic objectives and completely neglecting questions of Soviet response and strength.

The plan called for a phased offensive that would encircle and destroy the bulk of the enemy between the Donets and Don rivers, in the region west of Stalingrad. The precise fate of Stalingrad, a railway center and important port on the Volga River, was not clearly spelled out. The directive instructed only that, to protect the left flank of the main thrust into the Caucasus, every effort would be made "to reach Stalingrad itself, or at least to bring the city under fire from heavy artillery" so that it would no longer be of any use as an industrial or communications center. Yet, in the coming months, the effort to subdue Stalingrad would become not only the obsessive focus of the offensive but a turning point in the war.

As the Germans prepared for operation Blau, a number of battles flared up, from the Crimea in the south all the way north to Leningrad. Hitler's directive called for "mopping up and consolidation on the whole eastern front." The Russian high command, meanwhile, ordered local offensives as part of their strategy of an "active defense," thus putting their forces on a collision course with Hitler's preliminary operations.

Hitler wanted to clear out stubborn Soviet strongholds on the Crimean peninsula to secure his extreme southern flank and the back door to the Caucasus. The task fell to Army Group South's right wing, comprising the Eleventh Army and several Rumanian divisions under the overall command of General Erich von Manstein. On May 8, Manstein assaulted the eastern end of the Crimea from land and sea, launching a dramatic eight-week campaign that resulted in the capture of nearly 270,000 Russians and the successful siege of the fortress at Sevastopol (pages 40-57).

More than 1,000 miles to the north, meanwhile, the eight-month-old battle for Leningrad resumed. In late March, General Andrei A. Vlasov, a vigorous Soviet commander who had proved his mettle in the winter counteroffensive before Moscow, took over the stalled Second Shock Army, which had been cut off and trapped in the swamps along the Volkhov River during the drive to relieve Leningrad. Vlasov was ordered to smash through the German encirclement and get the 130,000 troops moving again.

Germans from Army Group North pressed in, hoping to tighten their grip on the Volkhov pocket, while Vlasov's army tried repeatedly to link up with Soviet forces attacking from the east. The Russian relief attempts would briefly break through to the pocket—on June 19, for example, a dozen T-34 tanks held open a supply corridor 150 yards wide during the night—only

The German army awarded a variety of combat badges to its troops. Infantrymen involved in at least three attacks on the enemy received the infantry assault badge; supporting troops such as artillerymen won the general assault badge. After downing at least four enemy planes, members of an anti-aircraft battery were rewarded with the army flak badge. The tank battle badge went to tank crews who fought in at least three separate engagements.

Infantry Assault Badge

General Assault Badge

Army Flak Badge

Tank Battle Badge

to see it slam shut. Vlasov himself refused to flee the pocket in an aircraft Moscow sent to rescue him.

On June 22, the pocket closed for the last time. Over the next week, some 33,000 Red Army soldiers, out of food and ammunition, surrendered; the remaining 100,000 men of the Second Shock Army were dead or dying. During the aftermath, a German patrol came upon Vlasov in a farm shed. Soon after he was captured, the heroic general did an about-face: He agreed to assume command of the Russian Army of Liberation, a puppet force being recruited by the Germans from prisoner-of-war camps. Vlasov's experience in the Volkhov pocket had proved so disillusioning that he was willing to take up arms to liberate his country from Stalin's dictatorship.

To the south, in the center of the front, German operations were limited to straightening out the meandering battle lines left by the winter's harsh combat. This sector was a maddening and tactically dangerous complex of bulges and pockets so convoluted that its straight-line length of 350 miles nearly tripled in actual configuration. On this front, Army Group Center put together three operations that netted nearly 50,000 prisoners by mid-July.

On another front, that of Army Group South, the arena for the upcoming offensive, the Germans mounted a preliminary operation to eliminate a troublesome bulge in the Soviet line. The Red Army salient protruded westward from the Donets River into a section of the German line where forces would be assembling for operation Blau. A legacy of the Russian advance during the winter, the bulge extended on either side of the river town of Izyum, north to Balakleya and south to Slavyansk, and westward for a distance of some sixty miles. The Izyum salient not only interfered with preparation for Blau; it represented a potential springboard for an attack on German-held Kharkov, some seventy-five miles northwest of Izyum. Kharkov, the Soviet Union's fourth largest city, was now a Wehrmacht supply center.

Plans to eliminate the salient had proceeded since March under the direction of Field Marshal Fedor von Bock, the commander of Army Group South. Bock had assumed command in January, a month after being relieved of Army Group Center in front of Moscow, ostensibly for reasons of health. The son of a general, Bock was the epitome of the old-line Prussian officer who aroused Hitler's ire. But the caustic and aristocratic field marshal had won high regard in previous campaigns, ranging from the annexation of Austria to the invasion of France.

On May 1, a day after Bock issued the final directive for Operation Fridericus, the attack on the salient, an ominous memorandum came down from the German high command's new intelligence chief for the eastern front, Lieut. Colonel Reinhard Gehlen. Based on information from

Captured on July 12, 1942, after a Russian defeat near Leningrad, the Soviet general Andrei Vlasov and a woman companion passively await their fate. German troops found the two hiding in a shed on a farm not far from the battlefield. Vlasov, shown under interrogation (*left*), agreed to become head of the Russian Army of Liberation, made up of Soviet prisoners of war who fought with the German army.

agents, intercepts of Russian broadcasts, and other sources, Gehlen's report warned of imminent Soviet *Zermürbungsangriffe*—"wearing-down attacks." In particular, Gehlen cited suspicious enemy troop movements in the Izyum salient and suggested the likelihood of a "Kharkov offensive." Gehlen was amiss only in his failure to grasp the scale of this action, for at that moment an enormous Russian force was gathering on the west side of the Donets. Into the Izyum pocket and a smaller bridgehead near Volchansk, eighty miles north of Izyum, were pouring no fewer than five Soviet armies comprising more than 640,000 men and 1,200 tanks.

The Russians struck on the morning of May 12, six days before the scheduled start of the German attack on the salient. After an hour of bombardment by the air force and the artillery, the Red Army commander, Marshal Semyon Timoshenko, unleashed three powerful columns of armor and infantry against the German Sixth Army. One column bore down upon Kharkov in a southwesterly direction from the Volchansk salient. The two other columns sprang out of the Izyum salient: one northwesterly toward Kharkov and the other westward toward the rail center of Krasnograd, sixty miles southwest of Kharkov.

The impact sent the Germans reeling. The Sixth Army reported that no fewer than twelve Soviet rifle divisions and 300 tanks had rammed its positions in the first waves. By noon, the German lines had broken on all three fronts. In the west, German and Rumanian divisions retreated in front of Krasnograd, threatening to open a gap in the communications between the Sixth Army in the north and Group Kleist in the south. That evening, Red Army tanks roamed northeast of Kharkov only a few miles from the city.

Faced with this peril, Bock telephoned the high command on the night of May 12. He told Halder that the Germans' own local offensive, Operation Fridericus, would have to be abandoned and troops redeployed to defend Kharkov. Halder, quoting Hitler, replied that there would be no redeployments for the repair of "minor blemishes." "This is no blemish," Bock retorted. "It's a matter of life and death!"

Two days later, as the attacking Russians punched even larger holes in his lines, Bock tried again. He proposed shifting three or four divisions from General Ewald von Kleist in the south to help the Sixth Army stall the Russian onslaught below Kharkov. But Hitler would have none of it. The Führer did promise help in the form of Stuka dive bombers to be shifted north from the Crimea, but he stubbornly insisted that Fridericus proceed even though a pincers attack, as originally planned, was now out of the question. With one of his pincers, the Sixth Army, tied up in the north, Bock would have to attack with only his southern arm—Group Kleist, which

consisted of the Seventeenth Army and Kleist's own First Panzer Army.

Bock launched his one-armed offensive at 3:00 a.m. on May 17. Hitler's feel for the situation proved remarkably prescient. Soviet spearheads were now only about thirty miles from Bock's headquarters at Poltava. But these columns were now stretched out for a length of seventy miles. They were far ahead of their supplies and vulnerable to Kleist, whose divisions slammed into their open flank from the south that morning.

Group Kleist fell on the Russians along a front nearly sixty miles long, from Lozovaya eastward to Slavyansk, near the Donets River. Among the infantry and panzer divisions leading the assault was a battalion of French-speaking Belgians known as Walloons. Formed as a volunteer legion, the Walloons, who would later be absorbed into the Waffen-SS, were operating as an independent unit attached to Lieut. General Eberhard von Mackensen's III Panzer Corps, the spearhead of Kleist's attack. Of the original contingent of 850 men recruited for the Walloon battalion in 1941, only 3 would survive the war.

On the morning of May 17, the Walloons demonstrated cleverness as well as courage. As they pressed forward through a small valley, approaching the village of Yablenskaya, they came under fierce artillery and machine-gun fire. Seeking cover, the Belgians threw themselves under the haystacks that abounded on the landscape. Then, to the astonishment of their colleagues watching through binoculars from the nearby hillside, the haystacks began to move.

"Like tortoises, they were advancing toward the enemy in furtive movements," wrote Leon Degrelle, the Belgian Fascist leader who served with the Walloons. "It was a spectacle that was as funny as it was exciting. The Russians could not machine-gun the valley indefinitely. With each respite, the haystacks moved forward several meters. There were many haystacks; it was almost impossible for the Russians to get their bearings and discover which were those that hid the advance of our sly companions."

The Belgians sweltered under the haystacks. But they kept inching forward, and after nearly two hours, many of them reached the cover of low ridges. Meanwhile, German artillery found the range, and an armada of more than sixty Stukas blasted the Russian positions around Yablenskaya. The tenacious resistance finally ended at three o'clock that afternoon. "Our soldiers then leapt from their haystacks," wrote Degrelle, "loath to accord anyone else the honor of entering the burning town first."

A company of Berliners from the 466th Infantry Regiment also resorted to unconventional tactics when they encountered fierce resistance on the morning of May 17. At first, the going was relatively easy, with Stukas paving their way. The regiment also had the support of self-propelled 20-mm

Infantrymen of the German Sixth Army trudge past a blazing village during fighting near Kharkov. The ferocity of the Soviet counterattack on May 12 stunned the German defenders south of the city. One German soldier wrote, "It looks like the enemy wants to stake everything on one throw."

antiaircraft guns of the 616th Army Flak Battalion. The 616th's gun crews accompanied the Berliners into combat right up on the front line, firing on ground targets at point-blank range with awesome effect. But minefields, thick undergrowth, fields strewn with felled trees, and concealed pockets of Russian soldiers slowed the advance.

The Berliners ran into an unusually stubborn defense on a collective farm called the Mayaki Honey Farm. To silence the nests of machine guns and mortars there, they called in artillery support. The message went back by radio, and a few minutes later, shells began to fall just in front of the farm. The barrage brought answering salvos from Red Army guns.

Through this shower of exploding metal, the Germans charged a Russian trench. "The Soviets were still in it, cowering against its side," one soldier wrote. "The charging German troops leapt in and likewise ducked close to the wall of the trench, seeking cover from the shells, which were dropping in front, behind, and into the trench. There they were crouching and lying

Called up from the rear to bolster the Sixth Army's battered line, exhausted soldiers of the 305th Infantry Division catch their breath during their forced march to Kharkov. German officers struggling to move men and equipment found a formidable obstacle in the region's rough and rutted terrain.

shoulder to shoulder with the Russians. Neither side did anything to fight the other. Each man was clawing himself into the ground. For that moment they were just human beings trying to save themselves from the murderous, screaming, red-hot splinters of steel."

A half-hour later, the artillery barrage ended abruptly, and with it the temporary truce in the trench. The Germans jumped to their feet, shouting "Ruki verkh!" ("Hands up!" in Russian), and disarmed their Red Army trenchmates. Resuming their advance, they soon found themselves in more felicitous circumstances. They came upon a cluster of ten Red Army field kitchens ready to serve a steaming breakfast. To the astonishment of the Russian cooks, the Berliners eagerly lined up, guns at the ready, to receive their unexpected fill of tea and millet porridge.

All along the front, Kleist's columns carved into the southern flank of the Russian corridor. On Kleist's left, the III Panzer Corps drove fifteen miles northward and reached Barvenkovo by sundown on the first day. On the right, the Seventeenth Army went even farther, covering more than two-thirds of the way to Izyum. While these spearheads threatened to cut off the seventy-mile-long Russian bulge at its base, delay and indecision plagued the Red Army. The Soviet commander, Marshal Timoshenko, had waited until that morning—too long—to throw in his substantial reserve of two tank corps. And they had been deployed to bolster the drive on Kharkov—too far to the northwest to blunt Kleist's surprise attack from the south. That night, Timoshenko shifted one of the tank corps to deal with the threat in his rear, despite Stalin's obstinate insistence on pressing the doomed offensive against Kharkov.

The second day of the German attack, May 18, turned into a near rout. Once again, the Luftwaffe played a pivotal role. True to his promise to Bock, Hitler brought up from the Crimea powerful squadrons of the VIII Air Corps to join the fighters, Stukas, and bombers of the IV Air Corps already present. The impact of this concentration of air power was dramatically brought home to a soldier named Benno Zieser and his comrades in a motorized infantry division. Mortar fire from the Russians was slowing their advance and beginning to inflict heavy casualties.

"At that point," wrote Zieser, "we got unexpected help. Three Stukas came roaring along, flying low, and banked two or three times at increasingly sharp angles. Then suddenly they came diving down, blazing away with all they had, and whizzed past just above our heads. Hundreds of tiny death-dealing flames spurted from their gun muzzles. Involuntarily, we pressed our faces into the soil. Our nerves were strained to the breaking point. Did they take us for Russians? But then we saw the tracers, striking home precisely where we reckoned the enemy would be. Our aircraft climbed high, hovered for a few moments, then again swooped down on the Russkies. The shooting opposite us ceased. Again, we were ordered to advance, but this time it did not strike the same terror in our hearts."

Ramming ahead under the Luftwaffe's canopy of steel on the second day, the Germans tore a forty-mile-wide gap in the Russian flank. Panzers and truck-borne infantry cleared the west bank of the Donets all the way north to Izyum, narrowing the Soviet corridor to a neck only twenty miles across. Now clearly in danger of having their westward thrust lopped off, the Soviet field command again appealed to Moscow. Not until the following night did Stalin relent and agree to call off the Kharkov offensive. By that time, Timoshenko, acting on his own, already had begun deploying his troops to counter Kleist on the southern flank.

The shift came too late to blunt Kleist's thrust from the south. Yet, at the same time, it suddenly relieved the pressure on the German Sixth Army in the north, allowing its commander, General Friedrich Paulus, to join in the

Crushing a Soviet Strike

On May 12, 1942, six days before the scheduled opening of Operation Fridericus, the German attack on the Izyum salient, the Soviets launched a powerful two-pronged offensive designed to encircle the Germans around Kharkov and retake the city. While the Twenty-Eighth Army struck at the German lines northeast of Kharkov, the Soviet Sixth Army and the Bobkin Group attacked north and west from the Izyum bulge. The German Sixth Army, which was supposed to be the northern fist of Fridericus, was hit hard, and Soviet spearheads were soon probing toward Kharkov and Krasnograd. With his Sixth Army in trouble, Hitler was compelled to order the southern arm of Operation Fridericus into action. On the morning of May 17, Group Kleist—consisting of the Seventeenth Army and the First Panzer Army—smashed through the perimeter of the salient and into the rear of the Russian attackers. As the Soviets turned to face this threat, the German Sixth Army counterattacked, checking the Soviet advance and linking up with Group Kleist to close the pocket on more than 240,000 Red Army troops.

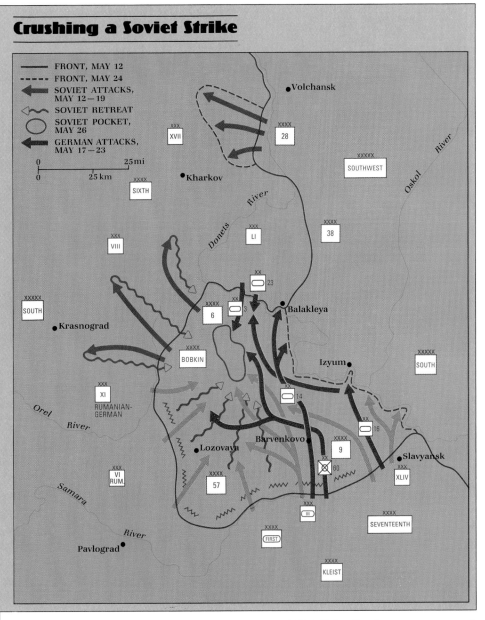

developing encirclement. Late on May 19, while Kleist further compressed the neck of the Izyum bulge to fifteen miles, troops under Paulus bore down from the north. Both of the pincers originally envisioned in Operation Fridericus were now in motion, threatening to entrap more than 200,000 Russians. "Now," Bock wrote in his diary the following night, "everything will turn out well after all!"

As the pincers closed, the panzer spearheads faced the same desperate tactics that they had encountered the previous summer. Russian soldiers, hidden in well-camouflaged positions, unleashed packs of dogs trained to run underneath tanks. The dogs carried on their backs explosives that detonated when projecting trigger rods came into contact with the vehicles. German riflemen accompanying the panzers picked off the dogs before they could do much harm, but the route of advance became littered with their dangerously mined carcasses.

The pocket clamped shut on the afternoon of May 22. Armor from Kleist's 14th Panzer Division reached the Donets south of Balakleya. From the far bank of the river, they were hailed by infantry of the Sixth Army coming down from the north. Their linkup, and the completion of a chain of armor the following morning ten miles to the west, sealed the encirclement.

As the Germans tightened the noose west of the Donets, Stalin refused to send reinforcements to relieve Timoshenko's beleaguered men. Afterward, General Paulus wrote to his son, Ernst, a panzer officer wounded in the battle: "A Russian officer who fell into our hands told us that Timoshenko himself became involved in one of the tank engagements and that when he saw with his own eyes how his forward troops, and particularly his tanks, were being literally shot to pieces, he exclaimed 'This is frightful!' and then, without another word, turned and left the battlefield." At length, entire formations of trapped Russians were reduced to attempting human-wave assaults. Night after night, by the light of German flares, thousands of Soviet soldiers fortified themselves with vodka, linked arms, and then flung themselves against the guns and panzers in futile efforts to break free. Others simply abandoned the fight and surrendered.

After the fighting ended on the morning of May 28, the Germans claimed more than 240,000 prisoners and over 1,200 tanks captured or destroyed. In the battles of encirclement fought within a three-week period here and in the Crimea, they had smashed six Soviet armies and captured 400,000 men. "We were buoyed up with new hope and confidence," a soldier later recalled. "I don't think there was one of us who wasn't convinced that we were winning the war. We were in a state of intoxication."

Hitler, too, felt confident. He was so pleased with developments in the south that on June 1 he flew to Bock's headquarters at Poltava to discuss the final plans for Blau. According to Paulus, who was in attendance along with other top commanders, the Führer made no mention of Stalingrad as an important objective but targeted two cities in the Caucasus, saying, "If we don't get Maikop and Grozny, I shall have to pack up the war."

Bock was less optimistic than his commander in chief. He expressed concern about reserve forces that the Red Army was concentrating behind the front. "And what do these reserves consist of," Hitler retorted. "Stupid cotton pickers from Kazakhstan, Mongolian half-apes from East Siberia, who will run away at the first rumble of a Stuka! I tell you, Bock, we have them by their coattails! The motto is: Attack! And attack again! This time there will be no severe winter weather to save them. We will be sitting in the Caucasus and operating their oil fields long before then!"

Bock's cautious approach angered Hitler. On the return flight to Germany, he confided to an aide his intention to retire the old field marshal after the war was won, declaring, "He is simply too old-fashioned to take part in our future plans."

The Kharkov battle had delayed preparations for Blau, and now Hitler decided to postpone it even further. To take advantage of the apparent Soviet disarray in the region and to secure better launching positions for the big offensive, the Führer ordered two more small-scale operations. The first, initiated on June 10, eliminated what was left of the Volchansk salient and established a bridgehead on the east bank of the Donets, northeast of Kharkov. The second attack, begun on June 22, cleared the area east of Izyum between the Donets and its tributary, the Oskol. These operations cost the Red Army an additional 47,000 prisoners and established advanced jumping-off points for Blau.

Hitler, meanwhile, had launched a campaign of deception to divert Soviet attention from the southern front. He wanted to convince the Russians that Moscow, rather than the Caucasus, would be the primary target of the summer offensive. To this end, Propaganda Minister Joseph Goebbels had his operatives run false stories in the German press and plant

Soviet soldiers move toward captivity after the last of more than 200,000 men surrendered near Kharkov on May 28. A German

directive ordered that "all prisoner resistance, even passive, be eliminated by the use of arms (bayonet, rifle butt, or firearm)."

rumors among foreign agents and reporters in the neutral city of Lisbon.

Meanwhile, Army Group Center, the headquarters responsible for the purported Moscow offensive, undertook a series of misdirection schemes code-named Operation *Kreml* (Kremlin). A bogus directive calling for "the earliest possible resumption of the attack on Moscow" was drawn up on May 29 over the signature of Field Marshal Günther von Kluge, the army group commander, and broadcast on a frequency monitored by Russian intelligence. German agents swarmed eastward carrying the news, and the Luftwaffe stepped up reconnaissance flights over the Moscow area. Kluge's commanders distributed maps and held planning conferences. His panzers staged such convincing preparations that only those few top officers privy to the secret knew the offensive was phony.

Operation Kremlin and the other schemes were effective because they played to the Soviet leaders' own suspicions. Although Hitler did not realize it, Stalin already half believed that the summer target would be Moscow. Hitler had tried it before, and Stalin thought he would try it again—as a head-on blow from Army Group Center or perhaps as an uppercut from Bock's Army Group South.

At the same time, Hitler made every effort to keep preparations for the actual offensive shrouded in secrecy. He forbade field commanders to commit their orders to writing and instructed them to convey only the barest minimum of oral orders to subordinates. Hitler was so bent on secrecy that even during the darkest moments of the Soviet offensive to retake Kharkov back in May, he had refused to send into battle the additional units being concentrated for operation Blau for fear that any premature troop movements into Army Group South's sector would tip off the Russians that something bigger was afoot.

Just as Hitler's mania for deception and secrecy seemed to be working, a violation of security by one of his best panzer generals threatened to unravel everything. The episode began on June 17 at a briefing conducted by Lieut. General Georg Stumme, the much-esteemed chief of the Sixth Army's XL Panzer Corps, who was known as Fireball because of his energetic demeanor and red face. Following Hitler's security orders, Stumme gave his division commanders oral rather than written instructions for the first phase of the offensive. But Stumme relented after one of the commanders begged him for "a few points in writing" to aid his memory. He dictated a half page of notes outlining the corps' role in the first days of operation Blau and sent a typed copy to each division headquarters.

This seemingly harmless breach of security turned serious two days later. On June 19, Major Joachim Reichel, the operations chief of the 23d Panzer Division, took off in a Fieseler Storch observation plane to scout the terrain northeast of Kharkov, where the division's regiments would be deployed. He carried with him the typed orders from General Stumme and a map denoting the positions of the corps' divisions and their initial objectives. The little plane strayed over Soviet territory, took a bullet in the fuel tank, and went down about two and a half miles behind enemy lines.

That same evening, Stumme learned of the missing plane at a lavish dinner party for his staff and division commanders. He was more alarmed about Reichel than about the missing documents; if Reichel fell into the hands of Red Army interrogators, they might force him to reveal everything he knew about operation Blau, including its ultimate objective in the Caucasus. Stumme's concern intensified after a German patrol came across the plane the following morning. They found no trace of the precious papers, but nearby graves turned up two bodies—presumably those of Reichel and his pilot; the corpses were in such poor condition that positive identification was impossible. The only thing that the Germans could ascertain was that the Russians had been there first.

The shock waves from the incident reverberated all the way to Hitler's Alpine retreat in Bavaria. The Führer, though momentarily unsure whether to cancel Blau now that the Russians might know about it, was certain of one thing: He would make an example of Stumme. To Hitler, the blunder was yet another example of disloyalty by the old officers' corps—"a case of outright disobedience," one of his aides told Bock, who was summoned to Wolfsschanze to answer for it. A hastily convened court-martial found Stumme and his chief of staff guilty of excessive disclosure of orders and sentenced them to imprisonment. However, the presiding officer, Reich Marshal Hermann Göring, persuaded Hitler to grant clemency, and both defendants were posted to Rommel's desert war in North Africa. Stumme, still the fireball panzer leader as Rommel's deputy, would die in action there in October at El Alamein.

Hitler, meanwhile, ordered Blau to proceed as planned. As it turned out, the Russians had recovered Reichel's papers and quickly passed them up the Soviet chain of command. Stalin himself studied the maps and Stumme's notes and read of the German intention to strike eastward toward the Don River and seize Voronezh, some 175 miles northeast of Kharkov. But the Soviet dictator's attention was now so firmly focused on Moscow that he dismissed the documents as a "big trumped-up piece of work by the intelligence people." Even so, it was possible to interpret a purported attack on Voronezh as the opening wedge in a drive against Moscow, and Stalin began stacking up forces in the area northeast of Voronezh, between that city and the capital.

Luftwaffe pilots and crews involved in combat missions were eligible for one of the three badges shown above. Bomber squadrons received a badge with a winged bomb pointing downward (top), while the prize for fighter crews featured a winged arrow (middle). An eagle's head embellished the award for reconnaissance and weather squadrons (bottom). Bronze badges went to airmen with at least 20 missions, silver to those with 60, and gold to men with 110 or more.

During the German advance across the vast Russian steppe, a tank crew of the 23d Panzer Division stops to watch as a shell

explodes in the distance. "The space was so immense," said one German, "that it made some of our soldiers melancholy."

The full plans for Blau were so complex that Stalin, seeing only a fragment of them, could be forgiven for thinking it all a ruse. The offensive called for a series of consecutive, interdependent attacks launched from north to south along a front centered roughly at Kharkov and extending from north of Kursk to the Sea of Azov. For these thrusts, Bock had available some sixty-five German divisions and twenty-five divisions from the Hungarian, Italian, and Rumanian allies—about one million men in all.

After the capture of Voronezh in the first phase, these separate columns would converge in an intricate series of maneuvers down the Don toward Rostov. They would trap and destroy the enemy forces in the great eastward bend of the river, then realign in two groups. While one group swept down the right bank of the upper Don to secure the army group's northern flank, the other would secure the lower Don and push on to Stalingrad. With the lower reaches of the Don and the Volga cleared of the enemy, they would then strike southward into the oil fields of the Caucasus.

The first stage of operation Blau began at daybreak on June 28. The northernmost wing, commanded by General Maximilian von Weichs, attacked from its positions northeast of Kursk toward Voronezh, some 100 miles to the east. Weichs had nearly twenty divisions, with his own Second Army on the left, the Hungarian Second Army on the right, and the Fourth Panzer Army—recently transferred from Army Group Center—in the middle.

The first day of Hitler's summer offensive was so smashingly successful that it recalled the initial blitzkrieg of Russia the year before. Stuka dive bombers caught the Soviets by surprise, swooping down on the forward positions while other bombers, shielded by fighters, struck Soviet rear areas all the way to the Don. The flat terrain was ideal tank country, and the Fourth Panzer Army, under the vigorous leadership of General Hermann Hoth, the unflappable fifty-seven-year-old commander the crews called Papa, stormed ahead in classic style. War correspondents accompanying the armored columns wrote lyrical reports of the *Mot Pulk*, or motorized square, with its trucks and artillery shielded by a steel wall of panzers.

Rolling easily across the grass-covered steppe, the panzers reached the railroad bridge over the Tim River before noon. The defenders had already lit the charge intended to demolish the bridge, but the Germans ripped it out and kept moving. At the Kshen River, ten miles farther along, they seized another bridge. By nightfall, when it had started to rain, motorcyclists and others in the vanguard were storming the village of Yefrosinovka, thirty miles from their starting point. They barely missed the headquarters staff of the Soviet Fortieth Army, who had pulled out minutes before.

Although rain and stiffening Russian resistance slowed this northern

Stampede to the Don

On June 28, 1942, Field Marshal Fedor von Bock, commander of Army Group South, launched the first stage of operation Blau, sending the two panzer corps of Hoth's Fourth Panzer Army east toward Voronezh. Two days later, Paulus's Sixth Army moved out from positions east of Kharkov. Contrary to German expectations, the Soviets retreated everywhere but in the approaches to Voronezh. The drive produced only one encirclement, west of Stary Oskol, where the Germans netted 70,000 prisoners. Hoping to trap more at Voronezh, Bock ordered Paulus to divert units of the XL Panzer Corps northeast toward the city while the rest of the Sixth Army moved southeastward toward the Don on the heels of the Soviets. The Germans swept into Voronezh on July 6, but Hitler blamed Bock for concentrating too much armor there and delaying the offensive into the Caucasus. On July 9, he split Bock's command into Army Groups A, under List, and B, under Bock. That same day, List's First Panzer Army drove on Millerovo, but once again few prisoners were taken. On July 15, an enraged Hitler vented his frustration by relieving Bock of his command.

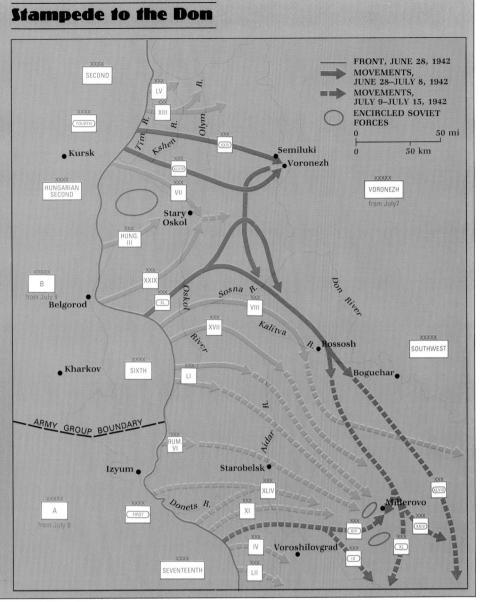

spearhead during the following two days, another powerful German thrust threatened Soviet defenses ninety miles to the south, in front of the Don. On the attack there was Paulus's Sixth Army, a formidable assemblage of fourteen divisions, including a pair of panzer divisions. Moving on the morning of June 30 from the Volchansk bridgehead northeast of Kharkov, the Sixth Army formed the right-hand pincer in the drive against Voronezh. Its orders were to slash eastward across the Oskol River and then dispatch its mobile formations to the northeast to hook up with Weichs's left-hand pincer descending on Voronezh.

At the forefront of Paulus's army rumbled Stumme's old XL Panzer Corps, still beset by the ramifications of Reichel's lost orders. Only three days before, replacements had arrived for Stumme and for the commander of Reichel's unit, the 23d Panzer Division. The Reichel mess aside, the men of the 23d may well have considered themselves snakebit. They were the new boys in the corps, recent arrivals from duty in France—a fact signified by the Eiffel Tower insignia on their vehicles. And they were shaken to realize that the enemy already knew of their presence, as was evidenced

Marder II Sd. Kfz. 131

Rising steeply above the five leaf-sprung road wheels characteristic of a Panzer II chassis, the Marder's lightly armored, partially enclosed superstructure shields a powerful 75-mm antitank gun. The Marder's open fighting compartment offered its crew of four only minimal protection; nevertheless, its mobility and hitting power filled a critical gap in the German arsenal.

Panzer IV F2 Sd. Kfz. 161

Jutting from the bowed mantelet on the turret, a 75-mm cannon extends forward of the hull, driver's visor, and MG 34 machine gun of this rearmed Panzer IV, which entered service in March 1942. Fitted with a single-baffle, spherical muzzle brake, the new gun made the tank nose-heavy and hard to steer, but its crews were glad to have the offensive power and range it provided.

Improvised Tank Killers

The Soviet T-34 tank appeared on the eastern front at a bad moment for the invading Germans. The T-34 was faster, heavier, and better armed than the Wehrmacht's largest operational tank, the Panzer IV, and Germany's next generation of armored fighting vehicles was still on the drawing board. Before 1941 ended, Hitler ordered his Weapons Department to beef up the existing armor in a hurry.

Ordnance crews fitted the Panzer IV with a long-barreled 75-mm cannon that could compete with the Soviet tank's superior 76.2-mm gun. The increased muzzle velocity and greater range of the new weapon enabled the Panzer IV, shown below, to hold its own against the T-34 until new German tanks could reach the battlefield.

Another serviceable product of wartime expediency was the Marder, the first effective *Panzerjäger*, or tank destroyer. To support the infantry, whose light, relatively immobile antitank weapons left foot soldiers all too vulnerable to enemy armor, the Germans mounted high-velocity 75-mm antitank guns (or, in some cases, captured Russian 76.2-mm guns) on the chassis of obsolete light tanks. The result *(left)* was a valuable stopgap tank killer.

by leaflets that showered from Russian planes. "We welcome you to the Soviet Union," said the leaflets. "The gay Parisian life is now over."

But the men of the 23d Panzer performed like veterans of the eastern front. Facing Russian forces that had lost their tanks during the battles around Kharkov the previous month, they and their comrades in the XL Panzer Corps smashed forward twenty miles that first day. On the following day, July 1, the vanguard crossed the Oskol and turned north, aiming for the river town of Stary Oskol, which was roughly halfway to the first main objective, Voronezh. On the Oskol, the Sixth Army was supposed to link up with the nearest elements of the Fourth Panzer Army from the north to form a small encirclement and trap Soviet forces still west of the river.

A strange thing happened as the two pincers closed in on Stary Oskol. The Soviet defenders, instead of standing fast as usual and fighting to the death or surrendering, were retreating. They were hurrying eastward—with Kremlin permission—to elude encirclement. Stumme's successor as commander of the XL Panzer Corps, Lieut. General Leo Geyr von Schweppenburg, was an old hand on the Russian front, and he quickly spotted this surprising change in enemy tactics. He asked for permission to wheel his corps eastward and race to the Don in hopes of blocking the retreat. The operation, however, went on as planned. On July 2, the pincers met, but large parts of two enemy armies had already crossed the Oskol River in full retreat eastward toward the Don.

The apparent change in Soviet tactics raised questions about the wisdom of the German intention to seize Voronezh. This city, which lay five miles east of the Don astride the smaller Voronezh River, was a vital armaments-making center and traffic junction. It commanded the crossings on both rivers as well as controlling communications by river, road, and rail between Moscow and the Black and Caspian seas. Capturing it had been thought essential to secure Blau's northern flank, and Hoth's Fourth Panzer Army was heading straight there "without looking to either side," as Bock wrote. Now, however, with the Russians in retreat, it occurred to the German commanders that their preoccupation with Voronezh might be a mistake. Would it allow the enemy to escape from the great bend farther south before Bock's panzers could sweep down the Don and cut them off?

Hitler, pondering the same matter, paid a surprise visit to Bock's headquarters at Poltava early on the morning of July 3. The Führer, who tended to alternate between arrogance and diffidence in dealing with his senior commanders, was in the latter state that day, despite having arisen at four o'clock in the morning for the long flight from his East Prussian headquarters. Hitler gave Bock a pleasant surprise by granting him freedom to resolve the Voronezh question as he saw fit. He could capture Voronezh

Sixth Army tanks and infantrymen (*below*) push on toward the Don River while wearier troops rest by the roadside. During the trek, a windmill (*right*) provided the only visual relief from a landscape that, according to one soldier, offered "no variety, no charm. A single severe tone dominated everything."

as planned, provided this did not unduly delay the movement of his armor down the Don, or simply bypass the city and "drive southward at once." Hitler was in a jovial mood, doubtless because the Crimean stronghold of Sevastopol had fallen that day. "He was obviously pleased with the progress of the offensive," Bock wrote. The Führer even joked about a recent change of command by the British in North Africa, remarking that the British

In July, using a pontoon bridge near Voronezh, a column of motorized artillery from the German Fourth Panzer Army rumbles east across the Don River past trucks and equipment abandoned by fleeing Russians.

tended to "saw off every general" for whom things did not go exactly right.

Bock recorded the remark in his diary but did not yet fully grasp its irony. After all, he appeared to be back in the good graces of the Führer who had dismissed him from the command of Army Group Center the previous December and who had more recently questioned the loyalty of Bock's subordinates during the affair of the lost orders. And by allowing him discretion in the matter of Voronezh, Hitler seemed to be easing his tight hold on the tactical reins.

After Hitler's departure, Bock momentarily hesitated about Voronezh. But the daring of his panzers soon decided the issue for him. On July 4, forward elements of the Fourth Panzer Army's 24th Panzer Division reached the Don, found a bridge that was still intact, and, daringly mixing in with retreating Russian units, roared on toward Voronezh. When Bock learned that his tanks were a few miles from Voronezh, he gave the order for them to finish the deed.

Later that day, the trailing flank divisions of the XLVIII Panzer Corps moved up to the Don in front of Voronezh. At the town of Semiluki on the northern flank, motorized infantry from the Grossdeutschland Division overcame counterattacks by T-34 tanks and reached a bridge that had not been blown. But bundles of dynamite were fixed to the span, and fire was sizzling along the fuse. A sergeant from the 7th Company of the division's Grenadier Regiment waded under the bridge and wrenched away the cord when the flames were only inches short of the explosives. His comrades hurried across to the east bank and formed a "reception committee" for Russian stragglers still crossing the span. The regiment's self-propelled assault guns then staged a reconnaissance in force and raced all the way to the railroad just north of Voronezh before pulling back in the face of furious counterattacks.

The buildup on the east bank of the Don continued against mounting opposition. By nightfall of July 5, Bock had elements of four divisions—one panzer, three motorized—on the outskirts of Voronezh, and the 23d Panzer Division from Paulus's Sixth Army was veering left to guard their southern flank. But the Soviets had massed substantial infantry and armor around the city—initially because Stalin still thought the German thrust was aimed at Moscow, then in a deliberate effort to gain time for his retreating columns to move safely across the Don farther south.

On July 6, savage fighting raged inside the city. From the Kremlin, 300 miles to the north, Stalin desperately directed the battle by telephone. On July 7, German radio prematurely reported the capture of Voronezh, but in fact Hoth's troops held only the part of the city west of the Voronezh River. His motorized infantry and their regular infantry replacements

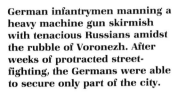

German infantrymen manning a heavy machine gun skirmish with tenacious Russians amidst the rubble of Voronezh. After weeks of protracted street-fighting, the Germans were able to secure only part of the city.

would hammer away for nearly a week and still not dislodge the defenders from the eastern section and its pair of vital north-south arteries—the railway and the highway.

Hitler, meanwhile, viewed the delays at Voronezh with growing impatience. He and Halder both realized they had allowed Bock to concentrate too many tanks in the north, a mistake that delayed the next phase of the operation: the combined sweep of armor down the Don to cut off the Russian retreat in the south. Now the telephone lines hummed between Hitler, Halder, and Bock. It was too late to quickly disengage the Fourth Panzer Army from Voronezh, but Hitler ordered the diversion of the XL Panzer Corps of Paulus's Sixth Army. These panzers, at least, were to turn south as originally planned and strike down the Don.

The corps began to pivot south on its rightmost element, the 3d Panzer Division, which was about fifty miles south of Voronezh on the night of July 6. The division's immediate objective lay another fifty miles farther south at the city of Rossosh, whose bridges spanned the Kalitva River. Although running short on fuel and ammunition, the 1st Battalion, 3d Rifle Regiment, started for the Kalitva that night with a battery of artillery and two companies of infantry in armored personnel carriers. "We knew that if the bridges over the Kalitva were to be captured intact," wrote the battalion commander, "we would have to reach Rossosh at dawn and would have to avoid all contact with the enemy, if only because of our shortage of ammunition and motor fuel. Thus, keeping rigidly to our timetable, we drove on, past advancing Russian artillery and infantry units who, luckily, did not realize who we were."

The little German column reached Rossosh as scheduled, at daybreak on July 7. Several of the vehicles rolled right past an unsuspecting Soviet sentry and across a bridge intended for tank traffic. But the sentry came to life when the battalion's command vehicle arrived moments later, and he brought his rifle to the ready. A radio operator jumped from the vehicle, poked his machine pistol into the Russian's stomach, and disarmed him. Just then, firing broke out. Soviet infantry and tanks attacked the Germans. Thanks largely to German gunners who concentrated fire from their battery of howitzers on the wide road along the river, the little contingent held out for nearly five hours until other units of the 3d Panzer Division arrived to relieve them before noon. Rossosh, it turned out, had been an important Red Army headquarters. The commander on this front, Marshal Timoshenko, had reportedly been there during the night but evidently had left in the early moments of the daring German foray.

Bock, under Hitler's strong proddings, managed to disentangle two of his mechanized divisions from Voronezh—the 24th Panzer and the Gross-

deutschland. But they were barely fifty miles from Rossosh when both had to stop for lack of fuel. West of Rossosh, one of Paulus's panzer divisions, the 23d, was similarly stalled. And the stubborn defenders around Voronezh continued to tie down the remainder of the Fourth Panzer Army.

Amid these disruptions of the timetable for Blau, the Germans finally launched a third parallel thrust eastward. On the morning of July 9, the vanguard began crossing the Donets south of Izyum, more than 100 miles southwest of Paulus's Sixth Army. This force was the new Army Group A—its core consisting of the Seventeenth Army and the First Panzer Army—commanded by Field Marshal Wilhelm List. List's new command signaled the division of Bock's Army Group South into two independent groups, as Hitler had previously planned, for the continuation of the offensive. Bock now commanded only Army Group B. To the old field marshal, the change not only diluted his authority, it was a tactical error as well. "This means that the battle is being chopped in two," he complained to his diary.

Field Marshal Fedor von Bock (*second from left*), in charge of the assault on Voronezh, reviews some of his troops. When Hitler removed him from command after the battle, Bock wrote, "There is no alternative but to face the fact that I have been made a monstrous scapegoat."

List's panzers, driving first northeast and then east to connect with Bock's armor coming down from the north, met little more than rearguard resistance; only at Voronezh was there heavy fighting. In the great bend of the Don that lay to the south of that city, the Soviets flocked eastward in full retreat. The lack of opposition troubled a correspondent for the Nazi party newspaper *Völkischer Beobachter*, who wrote: "The Russians, who up to this time had fought stubbornly over each kilometer, withdrew without firing a shot. It was quite disquieting to plunge into this vast area without finding a trace of the enemy." Hitler saw the Soviets eluding the encirclement snares he had laid for them and blamed Bock. The delay at Voronezh, he said, had prevented the panzers from getting down the Don in time to block the Soviet retreat. The Germans were failing in their primary aim, the destruction of enemy forces west of the Don; they had taken no more than about 70,000 prisoners during the first ten days of operation Blau. Hoping to trap more, the Führer departed from his plans and began improvising. Between July 10 and 12, he issued a series of orders for an intricate encirclement at Millerovo, about 150 miles east of Izyum, involving most of the armored and motorized units available to the two new army groups. In a telegram to Halder, Bock protested the plan as tactically unsound—strong in the center and weak on the flank. Since most of the enemy had already fled to the south and east, Bock predicted that Hitler's improvisation would result in a useless pileup of armor around Millerovo. Bock was right: The operation netted only around 50,000 prisoners.

But in Hitler's eyes, Bock had protested too much and delayed too long. On July 13, the Führer changed plans again. Convinced that large numbers of Russians were concentrated along the lower reaches of the Don, he abandoned the scheduled drive by all forces eastward toward Stalingrad and prepared a major encirclement by List's Army Group A around Rostov, 125 miles south of Millerovo. To spring the trap, he stripped Bock's Army Group B of the Fourth Panzer Army and gave it to List, leaving the Sixth Army as the only German force available on the northern flank. Then, virtually in the same breath, having developed "a distinct antipathy for Bock," as an aide later put it, he stripped Bock of his command.

Bock was ordered to turn over Army Group B to his commander on the northern wing, Maximilian von Weichs—again, a change ostensibly "for reasons of health." Such was the field marshal's prestige, however, that the Führer ordered the shift in command to take place in the strictest secrecy. For months, stories and photographs of Bock appeared in the government-controlled press as if he were still in command of the southern front in Russia. But the seasoned veteran, with forty-five years of military service behind him, would never command troops again. ✚

Target: The Crimea

In the spring of 1942, Hitler decided to complete the conquest of the Crimea, the 120-mile-long peninsula that provided the Soviet Union with important naval and air bases on the Black Sea. Although most of the Crimea had already fallen to German forces in the earlier stages of Operation Barbarossa, the Führer insisted that the last Soviet bastions be overcome before the Wehrmacht mounted its offensive eastward to Sta-

A Fieseler Storch reconnaissance plane skims over German motorized units advancing along the southern coast of the Crimea. Almost surrounded by the Black Sea and the Sea of Azov, the Crimean peninsula *(inset)* was largely open steppe with a southern mountain range and a rugged coastline that favored troops on the defensive. By the spring of 1942, the Russians had ringed the port of Sevastopol with fortifications and had forged a defensive line across the isthmus connecting the Kerch Peninsula to the rest of the Crimea.

lingrad and the Caucasus. The task fell to the 200,000 soldiers of the Eleventh Army, commanded by General Erich von Manstein, a rising star in the Wehrmacht.

Centuries of warriors from the ancient Scythians to the thirteenth-century Tatar khans had found the Crimea a tantalizing but often costly prize. During the Crimean War, Russian forces defended the peninsula against British and French armies in battles that in-

cluded the famous Charge of the Light Brigade and a bloody siege of the fortress city of Sevastopol.

By 1942, Sevastopol was widely regarded as the most heavily defended city in the world. Before tackling the city's garrison of more than 100,000 men, Manstein determined to deal with the other Soviet contingent on the Crimea: three armies deployed on the Kerch Peninsula at the eastern end of the Crimea.

A "Bustard Hunt" on Kerch Peninsula

On May 8, Manstein launched his drive against Kerch, called Operation Bustard Hunt after the large game bird that runs swiftly when endangered. The Soviet troops defending the eleven-mile-wide isthmus were thickly massed, their front spanned by a water-filled antitank ditch sixteen feet deep and thirty-three feet wide.

Manstein staged a feint against the Soviet defenses on the north flank. Then he launched the real attack on the southern end of the line with three infantry divisions aided by amphibious units that stormed ashore, hitting the flank and rear of the Russian defenses. The German troops routed the Soviets and established a bridgehead for the advance.

Spearheaded by the 22d Panzer Division, the Germans rolled up the Soviet line, then turned east as the enemy armies fled for the coast. Ten days after the attack began, the Kerch Peninsula was in German hands. The spoils of victory included some 170,000 prisoners and 1,133 artillery pieces.

German soldiers of the XXX Corps (*inset, top*) pause beside a captured Soviet trench before continuing the offensive.

Tanks of the 22d Panzer Division (*inset, bottom*) harassed the retreating Russians and mopped up pockets of resistance as the rest of the attack force swept on to Kerch.

After the guns of the XXX Corps thwarted a Dunkirk-like evacuation of the beleaguered Russian forces, the eastern tip of the peninsula (*main picture*) was strewn with wrecked and abandoned Soviet equipment.

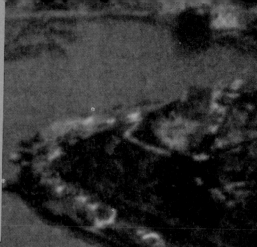

The assault on Sevastopol unfolded in two stages (*inset*). On June 7, the LIV Corps stormed the defensive belt north of the city and, after two weeks of bitter fighting, reached Severnaya Bay. On June 10, the XXX Corps attacked the Sapun Heights, clearing them in twelve days. Late in June, the attackers entered the city itself, where most resistance ended on July 3.

Smoke billows from Sevastopol's waterfront (*main picture*) during a massive German aircraft and artillery bombardment.

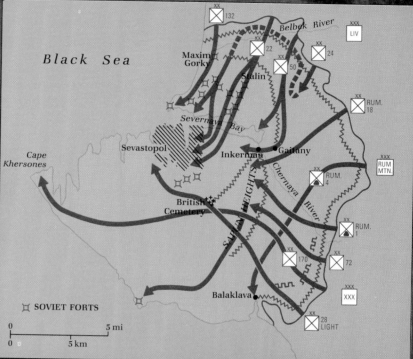

Siege of a Fortified City

Once Kerch had been cleared, Manstein embarked on what he called "the hardest task of all: the conquest of Sevastopol." The Crimea's largest city and the main naval base for the Soviet Union's Black Sea Fleet, Sevastopol was indeed a formidable fortress. Works that had withstood the bloody yearlong siege of 1854-55 during the Crimean War had been refined by generations of Russian military engineers. More than 100,000 Soviet troops and countless civilian volunteers had worked night and day for thirty weeks to further strengthen the city's defenses in preparation for the German onslaught.

Manstein's Eleventh Army would face a multilayered defensive network (*inset*). The outermost line was a deep maze of trenches and timbered strongpoints protected by minefields. Beyond this lay vast concrete forts linked by a labyrinth of tunnels, and barren hills covered with mortar emplacements and machine-gun nests.

On June 2, Manstein ordered his artillery to commence a five-day, round-the-clock bombardment as a preliminary to the assault. The planes of the VIII Air Corps, which held unchallenged control of the skies above the city, added their bombs to the inferno.

German artillerymen load a shell into the chamber of a heavy mortar *(inset, bottom)*, 576 of which were brought to bear on the Soviet defenses at Sevastopol.

Gunners race past another heavy mortar *(inset, top)* which is still smoking from its last round. The deafening noise of the exploding mortar shells caused panic among some Russian troops.

With a 107-foot barrel and an arsenal of five- and seven-ton shells, the giant railway gun nicknamed Dora *(main picture)* was the largest artillery piece in the history of warfare. More than 4,000 men were involved in transporting, guarding, maintaining, and firing the behemoth.

Mammoth Guns for Cracking Strongpoints

Manstein depended on his artillery to eliminate Sevastopol's vaunted defenses and clear the way for an infantry assault. With 208 batteries deployed over a twenty-two-mile front, "the Eleventh Army had called in every gun within reach," the general reported. "At no other time on the German side in World War II can artillery ever have been more formidably massed."

The biggest of the big guns was "Dora"—named for the wife of the Krupp engineer who designed it. Sixty railroad cars were required to transport the gun's components down a specially constructed spur to an emplacement nineteen miles from Sevastopol, a point still well within the weapon's twenty-nine-mile range. Once assembled, massive Dora weighed 1,488 tons and stood a towering 164 feet; its carriage, set on a double railroad track, was as large as a two-story house.

One of Dora's projectiles tore through ninety feet of solid rock before exploding and destroying an underground Soviet ammunition dump. But the weapon fared poorly against other targets since its shells tended to bury themselves deeply in the earth before detonating. Manstein later disparaged the value of his superweapon. "Undoubtedly, the effectiveness of the cannon bore no real relation to all the effort and expense that had gone into making it," he concluded.

Attacking "in the Spirit of Madness"

At daybreak on June 7, four German divisions stormed the Soviet lines north of Sevastopol, and it soon became clear that the bombardment had destroyed neither the Russian defenses nor the will of the defenders. German casualties mounted in what Manstein called "a bitter struggle for every foot of ground, every pillbox and trench."

The intrepid Germans forged ahead in a week of savage combat. "It was the spirit of madness," one German soldier recalled, "the desperation to seize an objective without regard to the cost."

On the seventh day of the offensive, the 16th Infantry Regiment took Fort Stalin, a key bastion in Sevastopol's inner ring of defenses. Every officer in the regiment was killed or wounded in the attack, and only four of the fort's defenders emerged from the demolished structure alive.

A German assault party *(inset, left)* in the Belbek Valley north of Sevastopol awaits orders to attack Soviet positions.

Charging Germans *(main picture)* bring a flamethrower to bear on a Russian pillbox. Even after artillery destroyed trenches and strongpoints, German infantrymen had to overcome defiant survivors with hand grenades, smoke canisters, and satchel charges.

Soviet dead lie in a ditch *(inset, right)*. Urged on by their officers and commissars, the Russians resisted with fanatical tenacity, many fighting to the death.

German soldiers *(inset)* take cover on the battered concrete face of Fort Maxim Gorky below the burning armored cupola with its two 12-inch naval guns, now crippled and askew.

At battle's end *(main picture)*, shattered chunks of the fort's concrete bulwark testify to the fierceness of the attack. When resistance ended, the Germans found only fifty Russian survivors, all severely wounded, in the bowels of the stronghold.

The Contest for Steel and Concrete

To claim Sevastopol, the Germans had to eliminate the fortresses that formed the backbone of the city's defensive system. Topped with heavy guns, these strongholds extended several stories underground and were equipped with power plants, water supplies, field hospitals, and arsenals.

The northernmost of the forts, Maxim Gorky I, commanded the Belbek Valley, a natural approach to the city, and was therefore a primary target. On the morning of June 17, German heavy mortars knocked out one of the fort's huge guns, and engineers demolished the other. The engineers then blasted a way through the thick concrete ramparts and began clearing the interior compartments with grenades, dynamite, and incendiary oil. The Russian garrison of a thousand men fought bravely until only a handful were left to carry on. That afternoon, the remaining combatants blew themselves up rather than surrender.

"Don't Believe Ivan Is Dead"

On June 10, three days after the main German thrust got under way in the north, General Maximilian Fretter-Pico's XXX Corps began its drive against the eastern front of the Sevastopol defenses. The rugged terrain in this sector impeded the Germans; nevertheless, by June 17, the outlying Soviet positions were in their hands.

Now the attackers faced the Sapun Heights, a natural bastion honeycombed with tunnels and concealed gun emplacements. The heights commanded the entire eastern front, and the Soviets defended the position with almost superhuman bravery. "Don't believe Ivan is dead just because his legs are blown off, his scalp is half torn away, and somebody has stuck a bayonet through his guts," one German noncommissioned officer warned. "If he has an arm left and a rifle within reach, he'll roll over and shoot you in the back as soon as you're past him."

On June 28, the Germans captured the stronghold of Inkerman, the northern anchor of the Sapun Heights, where thousands of Russians had sheltered in cliffside caves once used to store bottles of champagne. Much of the Sapun high ground, however, still remained in Soviet hands.

Troops of the German 170th Division surge forward in the assault on the Sapun Heights *(main picture)*. The German attack was slowed by numerous minefields and enfilading fire from cleverly camouflaged trenches and machine-gun nests.

Two German infantrymen *(inset, left)* fire into a Soviet foxhole. The Germans had to rout out each hidden Soviet position on the heights, often at point-blank range.

Droves of Soviet captives *(inset, right)* descend a ridge, bound for prisoner-of-war compounds behind the German lines.

A Surprise Strike by Assault Boat

By the third week of the offensive, German casualties were mounting, while the Soviets resisted as determinedly as ever. With most of the Sapun Heights and the city of Sevastopol yet to be taken, Manstein decided the time had come for a bold stroke to break the deadlock. On the north, the Germans had captured the concrete fortresses and had reached the north shore of Severnaya Bay. From there, at 1:00 a.m. on June 29, two infantry divisions would launch an amphibious assault across Severnaya Bay and into Sevastopol itself.

The general's subordinates were skeptical. Half a mile in width, the bay had a southern shore dominated by a cliff from which dozens of batteries and machine guns could bring their fire to bear on the water below. But Manstein insisted. "For the very reason that it appeared impossible," he later wrote, "an attack across Severnaya Bay would take the enemy unawares."

The plan worked to perfection. Under cover of darkness, assault boats bore troops of the 22d and 24th divisions to the south shore unopposed. By the time the Soviets realized what was happening, the Germans had entered Sevastopol.

Having fought their way to within sight of Sevastopol (*inset*), German infantrymen sheltering in a shallow trench on the northern shore of Severnaya Bay watch the city being bombarded.

Habitually close to the action, General Manstein, flanked by subordinates, observes the final assault on Sevastopol from an observation post overlooking the embattled Russian perimeter.

Valorous Resistance to a Bitter End

As the German noose tightened on Sevastopol, the remaining Soviets, responding to Stalin's orders to fight to the death, struggled in vain to hold their ground. Even the British Crimean War cemetery had been turned into a Soviet strongpoint. "The new dead," Manstein wrote, "were lying over graves torn open by shelling." In a final, despairing effort to break free of the trap, thousands of Soviets—soldiers, women, and children—linked arms and charged forward in suicidal human-wave assaults.

By July 4, the last pockets of resistance on the Khersones Peninsula west of the city were being wiped out, and the entire Crimea was in German hands. Three days earlier Hitler had elevated General Manstein to the rank of field marshal. The victors could claim nearly 100,000 prisoners and "booty so vast," Manstein said, "it could not be immediately calculated."

A German half-track rolls through the rubble-strewn streets of Sevastopol in the wake of Manstein's decisive victory. Hitler paid tribute to the "heroic achievements of the troops" under Manstein's command and ordered that a special badge *(inset)* be issued to veterans of the Crimean campaign.

War of the Rats

itler flew east on July 16, 1942—the day after his deposed commander, Field Marshal Fedor von Bock, took a westbound plane home to enforced retirement. The Führer and his military entourage established a new forward headquarters that morning on former enemy ground in a pine forest near Vinnitsa in the Ukraine. His decision to relocate from Wolfsschanze in East Prussia to this cluster of log cabins and wooden huts deep in the Soviet Union reflected his certainty that at last the Wehrmacht was moving in for the kill.

Hitler radiated confidence despite his discomfort. In the crude camp that he christened Wehrwolf, the stifling heat and humidity and the stench rising from the newly creosoted wooden planks gave him splitting headaches. But the headlong retreat of the Russians before the panzers now scouring the lower reaches of the great bend in the Don River persuaded him that his stay would be a short one. "The Russian is finished," he boasted to the chief of the army high command, Franz Halder. "I must admit, it looks like it," Halder assented, while complaining to his diary about the Führer's "chronic tendency to underrate enemy capabilities."

Hitler's rosy view of a Red Army on its last legs resulted in a stream of orders and directives whose execution would put a severe strain on German strength in southern Russia. Virtually on the eve of renewing the offensive in the south, he announced plans for robbing this front of no fewer than nine divisions. Two elite divisions of motorized infantry, the Grossdeutschland and the Leibstandarte SS, were to be redeployed in France to allay his developing fears of an Allied invasion. A pair of panzer divisions, the 9th and the 11th, were diverted to Army Group Center. And five additional divisions—the main body of Manstein's victorious Eleventh Army in the Crimea, standing ready to strike across the Kerch Strait into the Caucasus—were sent a thousand miles away to reinforce Army Group North for what the Führer expected would be the final, decisive offensive against Leningrad, scheduled for late summer. Most of all, however, Hitler's confidence was reflected in his revised plans for the final phases of op-

During the German push for the oil refineries and ports on the Black Sea in July 1942, mountain troops and their mules travel through the Klukhori Pass, a cleft 9,239 feet high in the western portion of the snowcapped Caucasus Mountains. Since there were only three good roads through the craggy range, the Germans often resorted to pack animals for carrying supplies.

The Drive into the Caucasus

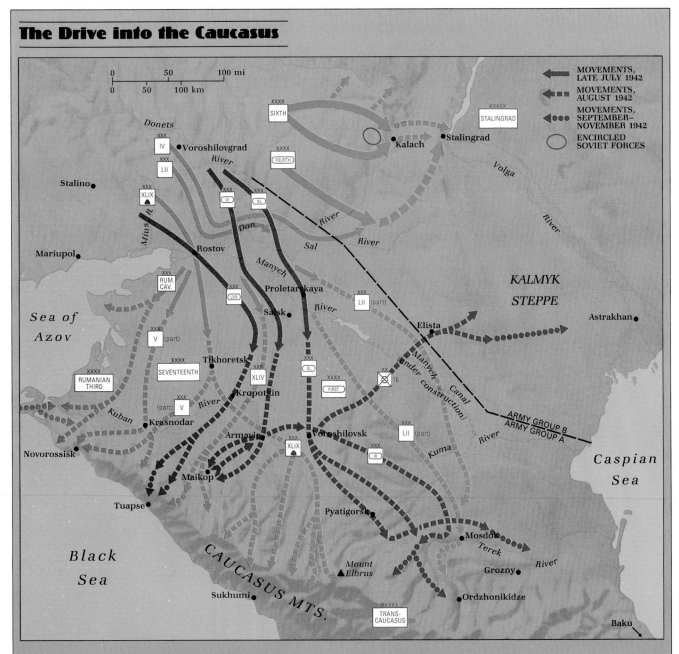

MOVEMENTS, LATE JULY 1942
MOVEMENTS, AUGUST 1942
MOVEMENTS, SEPTEMBER–NOVEMBER 1942
ENCIRCLED SOVIET FORCES

0   50   100 mi
0   50   100 km

Donets

SIXTH

STALINGRAD

IV
Voroshilovgrad

River

FOURTH

Stalino

Kalach

Stalingrad

Volga River

LII

XLIX

III

XL

Mius R.

Don

River

Mariupol

Rostov

Sal

River

River

Manych

RUM. CAV.

Proletarskaya

LVII

KALMYK STEPPE

Salsk

River

LII (part)

Astrakhan

Sea of Azov

V (part)

Elista

Tikhoretsk

SEVENTEENTH

XLIV

XL

Manych Canal (under construction)

RUMANIAN THIRD

Kropotkin

FIRST

16

ARMY GROUP B
ARMY GROUP A

V (part)

River

Kuban

Krasnodar

Armavir

Voroshilovsk

LII (part)

River

Caspian Sea

Novorossisk

XLIX

III

Kuma

Maikop

Tuapse

Pyatigorsk

Mosdok

Terek

River

Grozny

Black Sea

Mount Elbrus

CAUCASUS MTS.

Ordzhonikidze

Sukhumi

TRANS-CAUCASUS

Baku

In mid-July, as the Red Army fell back to the south and east, Army Group A, consisting of the Seventeenth Army and the First Panzer Army, secured Rostov and plunged into the Caucasus, with the Fourth Panzer Army of Army Group B supporting its left flank. Further north, the Sixth Army headed directly for Stalingrad. On July 25, Hitler ordered the Fourth Panzer Army to swing northeastward toward Stalingrad, splitting his two army groups and putting further strain on already precarious supply lines. During August and early September, the Germans made progress. On the right, the Seventeenth Army took Krasnodar and the Soviet naval base at Novorossisk. In the center, the Germans overran the oil fields at Maikop and pressed on to Tuapse, while farther eastward mountain troops moved into the Caucasus passes leading to the Black Sea coast around Sukhumi. The First Panzer Army on the left drove to the Terek River, in preparation for an assault on the oil fields at Grozny. But the German surge was peaking. Hampered by inadequate air support and dwindling fuel and ammunition, Army Group A slowed to a crawl in the face of stiffening Russian resistance. When List requested permission to dig in for the winter, Hitler fired him and took over command of the army group himself.

eration Blau. Under the new scheme, his forces in the south would be asked not only to complete the previous objectives of the summer offensive but to undertake ambitious new missions as well. Wilhelm List's Army Group A, in addition to capturing the vital oil fields of the Caucasus, was to occupy "the entire eastern coastline of the Black Sea, thereby eliminating the Black Sea ports and the enemy Black Sea fleet." Maximilian von Weichs's Army Group B, meanwhile, would no longer be relegated to the secondary role of driving eastward toward Stalingrad to guard the left flank of the thrust into the Caucasus. It was now entrusted with the outright capture of Stalin's namesake city.

Hitler's new directive flew in the face of conventional military doctrine. His two army groups on the southern front would have to diverge at right angles, opening a large and vulnerable gap between them and necessitating separate lines of supply. As the recently departed Bock had foreseen, the battle was being "chopped in two."

The first success in this double-pronged campaign was scored by List's Army Group A driving south. Even as Hitler issued his directive, the group's panzers and infantry were fighting in the streets of Rostov. By virtue of this city's location at the mouth of the Don near the Sea of Azov, Rostov was a gateway to the Caucasus, and the Russians fought a fierce delaying action. The Germans had to battle house-to-house in what one regimental commander termed a "merciless struggle" against fanatical troops of the NKVD, Stalin's dread secret police.

For the first time in Russia, the Wehrmacht had to endure the perils of street-fighting. NKVD troops barricaded the streets with paving stones, mined the alleys, sniped from rooftops and balconies, and hurled Molotov cocktails—bottles of gasoline fused with phosphorus or other chemicals that burst into flame upon contact with air. After two days of intense combat, German infantrymen cleared the road to the main bridge over the Don by bringing up antitank guns. Their task was to blow away—"shave off," in the words of one battalion commander—balconies, chimneys, and other structures that might harbor the enemy. By July 25—two days after the issuance of Hitler's new directive—the Red Army had retreated across the Don, and German engineers were establishing bridgeheads for the invasion of the Caucasus.

In the waning days of July, Army Group A marched southward across the Don in two main columns on a front nearly 100 miles wide. The right wing, crossing at Rostov, comprised Richard Ruoff's Seventeenth Army and the Rumanian Third Army. The left wing, breaking out from bridgeheads farther east, consisted of Ewald von Kleist's First Panzer Army. Kleist had 400 tanks and, on his left, the help of two divisions of panzers from Hermann Hoth's Fourth Panzer Army, the rest of which Hitler decided to divert on July 31 to the drive against Stalingrad.

As they plunged into the Caucasus, the Germans faced enormous distances and a landscape of extraordinary extremes. The farthest oil fields, at Baku, near the Caspian Sea, lay some 700 miles in a straight line southeast from Rostov—a distance farther than the German advance from the Soviet border to Rostov, which had required no less than thirteen months to complete. In between loomed the Caucasus Mountains, a chain 700 miles

After capturing Rostov, exhausted German soldiers push south across a pontoon bridge straddling the Don River.

A German gun crew loads a 75-mm antitank gun during fierce fighting in Rostov late in July. A German officer wrote, "The defenders would not allow themselves to be taken alive; they fought to their last breath; and when they had been bypassed unnoticed, or wounded, they would still fire from behind cover until they were killed."

long with peaks up to 18,000 feet high. Before reaching this formidable obstacle, the German columns had to traverse 300 miles of changing steppe that gradually evolved toward the south and east from fertile and well-watered granary into harsh desert, with practically no railroads or roads worthy of the name.

All the same, Field Marshal List found much cause for optimism. The enemy in front of him consisted of remnants of half a dozen Soviet armies already shattered north of the Don. The Russians were still retreating—"in wild flight," reported the First Panzer Army—despite special orders from Stalin on July 28 bluntly titled "Not a step backward." List's larger concern was fuel, which had to be airlifted to his fast-moving columns. The situation seemed so favorable on August 4 that, looking ahead to his ultimate objective 700 miles distant, he predicted, "A fast thrust to the southeast with sufficient mobile forces will not encounter serious enemy resistance anywhere forward of Baku."

All along the Caucasus front, events were bearing out List's optimism. On the left, about fifty miles south of the Don, his panzers successfully overcame a major obstacle in the form of the Manych River, which emptied into the lower Don. The Manych featured a series of dam-controlled reservoirs up to a mile wide. The retreating Red Army made crossing the river even more difficult by opening the floodgates of the dams and digging in on the south bank. But the men of the 3d Panzer Division cleared all hurdles. While German artillery suppressed enemy fire, the soldiers paddled across the

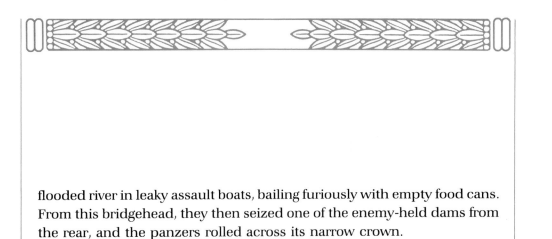

flooded river in leaky assault boats, bailing furiously with empty food cans. From this bridgehead, they then seized one of the enemy-held dams from the rear, and the panzers rolled across its narrow crown.

The division pushed southward into the arid wastes of the Kalmyk Steppe through scorching heat. Tanks and trucks stirred up such dense clouds of dust that from the air it was impossible to tell friend from foe. The Germans raced ahead under orders not to fire at enemy aircraft and

Black smoke billows from burning oil tanks near the town of Maikop during the German advance into the Caucasus in early August. By destroying oil and wrecking equipment, withdrawing Russians rendered the refineries useless to the German attackers. The region's oil fields had produced most of the Soviet Union's crude oil.

thus give away their identity. Otto Tenning, a signalman in the division, later recalled that men on the ground had trouble identifying even nearby objects through the curtains of dust. He was on a reconnaissance mission near a small village when the leader "suddenly spotted something suspicious and sent a radio signal: 'Enemy tanks lined up along the edge of the village.' To our surprise, we discovered a little later that these supposed tanks were in fact camels."

The panzers hurried on at a breakneck pace, hoping to catch the Soviets before they could leave the open steppe and take a stand in the mountains. The Germans covered so much ground that List had to wheel around two infantry divisions and deploy them eastward to protect the lengthening left flank of his armor. Although the Russians continued to elude them, the 3d and 23d Panzer divisions gobbled up the steppe. On August 10, they captured the town of Pyatigorsk, 250 miles south of the Don, and rumbled into the foothills of the Caucasus.

To the west, meanwhile, in the center of the advance, the right wing of the First Panzer Army bore down upon the oil fields at Maikop, 180 miles below the Don. Kleist's columns stormed across the Kuban River on August 5 and, reaching the railway, seized no fewer than fifty-one Red Army supply trains. Then they raced toward Maikop, guided by the giant flames that leaped thousands of feet into the sky as the Soviet rear guard set fire to the refineries and storage tanks. Late on August 9, the 13th Panzer Division entered the smoky haze enveloping the town.

Even the footslogging infantry of the Seventeenth Army made impressive progress during these early days of August. Marching past dazzling fields of man-high sunflowers that stretched to the horizon, the men covered up to thirty miles a day, stopping periodically to gorge on tomatoes, melons, and other produce that flourished in the fertile valleys north of the Kuban. "Our advance was so rapid that we needed new maps each day," an officer wrote later. "Indeed, special vans had been attached to our column to print maps as quickly as the offensive unrolled."

On August 9, after advancing nearly 200 miles from Rostov in two weeks, lead elements of the Seventeenth Army reached their first main objective: Krasnodar, on the north bank of the Kuban. Four infantry divisions moved up and, in 100-degree heat and a swirling dust storm, attacked the city. The Russian rear guard waged a furious delaying action to enable their men and equipment to escape across a bridge. At noon on August 11, the Germans battled to within twenty yards of the bridge, which was still choked with Soviet traffic. Just at that moment, a Russian officer set off explosives strapped to the pilings. The span collapsed at a half-dozen points, hurling Russian soldiers, horses, and vehicles into the water but also disrupting

German hopes for a major entrapment. The 125th Infantry Division finally managed to cross the river two days later by boat and raft and hook up with a column of Kleist's panzers swinging westward—but the retreating Russians had once again eluded the entrapment.

In mid-August, List regrouped his forces for the second phase of the campaign. To meet Hitler's multiple objectives, he augmented his right wing, the Seventeenth Army, with a panzer corps from the First Panzer Army on the left wing, and then sent his forces on diverging paths.

On August 17, the Seventeenth Army broke up into three columns, each with its own objective along the Black Sea. Infantry of the V Corps headed for Novorossisk, the northernmost Soviet naval fortress on the east coast of the Black Sea. The LVII Panzer Corps was to thrust southwest on the mountain road from Maikop to the port of Tuapse. The two divisions of the XLIX Mountain Corps were to cross the passes of the Caucasus south of Armavir and descend upon the coastal city of Sukhumi, some 100 miles north of the Turkish border. At the same time, on the German left, the First Panzer Army was to proceed southeast, seize the oil fields at Grozny, breach the mountains, and roll on to Baku.

In light of his earlier successes, List expected to control the Black Sea coast and have panzers on the Caspian Sea by the end of September. But the tempo of the campaign changed abruptly during the last two weeks of August. Concerned about Army Group B's drive on Stalingrad, Hitler diverted much of List's air support to that operation. Also, List's supplies were now chronically short. And with good reason: The Wehrmacht's lifeline on the southern front consisted of a single railway running eastward from the Donets Basin. Supplies were off-loaded and trucked to the four far-flung wings of Army Group A in the Caucasus, and to Army Group B in front of Stalingrad. Since airlift and truck transport were scarce, the Germans were reduced to hauling fuel by camel caravan. Meanwhile, Soviet resistance stiffened.

By the end of August, List's formerly fast-moving columns measured progress in terms of a mile or two a day, and he was beginning to talk about taking up winter positions. On his left, the First Panzer Army clung to a precarious bridgehead across the Terek, a broad and treacherous mountain river 60 miles from Grozny and 350 miles from Baku. On his right, only a contingent of Rumanian cavalrymen had reached the Black Sea coast, and they were well northwest of Novorossisk.

Alone among his diverging columns, the mountain troops achieved new distinction. Pouring into the heights south of Armavir, men of the 1st and 4th Mountain divisions seized several passes nearly two miles high that the

Dressed for the heat, a German soldier leads a camel through the desertlike steppe southeast of Rostov. Lack of fuel for trucks forced the Germans to rely upon horses, mules, and camels for transportation. One soldier recalled, "Camels were no longer anything unusual."

Red Army had considered impregnable. The Germans were aided in the task by former Red Army POWs: Kalmyks, Chechens, and other indigenous soldiers who had been taken captive earlier in the war. These men served as guides and helped bring the Germans a warm welcome from their countrymen, most of them Muslims who detested communism. (Stalin was so concerned about the loyalty of the inhabitants of the Caucasus that he dispatched Lavrenty Beria, the notorious chief of the secret police, in an attempt to keep them in line.)

To top off their success, the Germans scaled glacier-clad Mount Elbrus, the highest peak in the Caucasus, and planted the Reich battle flag on its 18,510-foot-high crest. After negotiating more than 100 miles of high terrain, however, the mountain troops ran low on ammunition and other supplies, as well as mules. Just a dozen miles short of their coastal objective, Sukhumi, their brilliant thrust stalled.

It was the deployment of the mountain troops that helped trigger a furor back at Hitler's new headquarters near Vinnitsa. Hitler had watched with mounting displeasure as the momentum of his Caucasus offensive began to wane. Then the exploit of planting the swastika on Mount Elbrus, a patriotic gesture that once would have warmed his heart, set the Führer raging about "those crazy mountain climbers." He even complained to his aides because List, when summoned to Vinnitsa by air to explain his plans,

brought with him an unmarked map. In this, Hitler conveniently overlooked his own standing orders that no marked maps be carried on aircraft, which he had issued after the plans for operation Blau had been lost to the Russians in the Reichel affair back in June.

Hitler differed with List on a number of tactical issues. But what irritated him the most was the field marshal's desire to withdraw his mountain troops from the passes leading to Sukhumi and concentrate them with his panzers to the northwest in the drive against Tuapse. On September 9, the Führer dismissed List and took personal charge of Army Group A, adding this responsibility to his other military burdens as commander in chief of the armed forces.

Men from Germany's **XLIX Mountain Corps struggle across a glacier on the slope of Mount Elbrus, at 18,510 feet the highest peak in the Caucasus range; the domelike, aluminum-skinned Intourist House, a Soviet hotel, is visible in the background. On August 21, in heavy snow and fog, the troops plant the German battle flag on what seemed to be the summit** *(above, right).* **Days later, when the weather cleared, they discovered that the flag actually flew from an eminence 130 feet below the peak.**

The firing of List was only the beginning of the crisis at Vinnitsa. Lieutenant General Alfred Jodl, Hitler's able, but usually compliant, chief of operations for the armed forces high command (OKW), had sided with List, a friend and fellow Bavarian. This act of perfidy by Jodl set the Führer against his top military men for the first time. For months, he refused to shake hands with either Jodl or Field Marshal Wilhelm Keitel, the servile OKW chief of staff. He retreated to his hut and took his meals alone there. To prevent any question arising about what was said in conversations with his generals, he brought in a team of stenographers to take down every word—a compilation that averaged some 500 typed pages a day.

In this atmosphere of distrust, it was not long before Hitler dealt with Franz Halder. With the recent departures of Bock and List, the chief of the army high command was one of the few remaining relics of the old officers' corps so detested by Hitler. The ties between the cerebral Halder and the impulsive Hitler, stretched thin for months, had frayed beyond repair a few weeks before when the two clashed over the question of a minor tactical withdrawal in Army Group Center.

"You always seem to make the same suggestion—retreat!" Hitler had snapped. "I must demand the same toughness from my commanders as from my troops." Halder lost his temper and lashed out at Hitler for the loss of "fine riflemen and lieutenants by the thousand" because local commanders were not given the freedom to pull back when necessary. The Führer then taunted Halder for his lack of combat experience, in contrast to Hitler's own front-line duty during World War I: "You who were as chairbound in the Great War as in this—what do you think you can teach me about the troops! You, who haven't even got a wound badge on your uniform!" Hitler ranted on, pounding the insignia on his chest.

On September 24, he dismissed Halder, who then wrote in his diary: "My nervous energy is used up and his is not as good as it was." Halder's replacement was General Kurt Zeitzler, the forty-seven-year-old chief of staff of an army group in western Europe. In contrast to his tall, slim, and professorial predecessor, Zeitzler was short, rotund, and so energetic that he was nicknamed Thunderball. Hitler hoped he would provide both unquestioning obedience and "National Socialist ardor."

Neither Zeitzler's enthusiasm nor Hitler's new leadership of Army Group A could compensate for the group's desperate needs for supplies, reinforcements, and air support. With the summer momentum gone, autumn of 1942 brought only local gains. On the German right, Seventeenth Army infantry occupied the northern Black Sea port of Novorossisk but failed to break out down the coast to Tuapse. Panzer and mountain troops trying to take Tuapse in an attack along a mountain road from Maikop were stopped a half-dozen miles from the sea. Farther south, mountain troops abandoned the advance against Sukhumi when supplies no longer could get through the snowbound passes. On the German left, 200 miles eastward, the First Panzer Army struck across the Terek River to within five miles of the foothill town of Ordzhonikidze before pulling back. Except for reconnaissance missions, German troops in the Soviet Union had reached no point farther east—but the town was still fifty miles short of the objective of Grozny, with its valuable oil fields.

By mid-November, when rain and snow ended operations, Hitler had grown increasingly distant from his command in the Caucasus. He had shifted his headquarters from Vinnitsa back to East Prussia, 800 miles from the front, and practically all his attention now focused on the epic struggle being waged for the city of Stalingrad.

The offensive against Stalingrad, unlike the strike southward into the Caucasus, had begun slowly. Back in July, the panzer spearheads of Weichs's Army Group B, assigned to move on Stalingrad, had stalled for ten days while the high command accorded priority for fuel and other supplies to the swift move into the Caucasus.

In early August, however, Sixth Army panzers were on the move again. They executed a classic double envelopment in the great bend of the Don and finally caught up with a large force of the retreating enemy. The pincers closed on August 7, when the XIV and XXIV Panzer Corps met on the west bank of the Don, opposite Kalach. They trapped about 1,000 tanks and other armored vehicles and more than 50,000 Soviet troops who evidently had heeded Stalin's injunction to take "not a step backward." It was the big battle of encirclement that Hitler had envisioned in planning operation Blau and the first actually accomplished since Kharkov back in May. During the following two weeks, the Germans methodically cleaned out the pocket and then established bridgeheads across the Don in preparation for their campaign against Stalingrad, forty miles to the east.

With its eighteen divisions, Sixth Army was the most important component of Army Group B. Its commander, Friedrich Paulus, overshadowed his superior, Weichs, because of Hitler's increasing tendency to intervene and deal directly with the general in the field. The fifty-two-year-old Paulus was a rising star in the Führer's eyes. He was a Hessian who had emerged from middle-class beginnings instead of from the aristocratic officers' caste, and he openly admired Hitler's military judgment. As a staff officer, he had helped plan Barbarossa, and Hitler had praised his handling of the Sixth Army during the fighting around Kharkov. Meticulously groomed—he bathed twice a day and wore gloves in the field to guard against dirt—he was also a methodical thinker who mulled over every alternative. He was tall and darkly handsome, and his first chief of staff was struck by the odd realization that Paulus had "the face of a martyr."

The plan worked out by Paulus and Weichs called for the deployment of forces to protect the army group's left flank stretching northwest for more than 200 miles to above Voronezh. These formations included the German Second Army and armies from Italy, Hungary, and—in September—Rumania. With his Sixth Army, Paulus intended to strike eastward with armor on both wings and infantry in the middle to "hit the Russian so hard a crack" that he would not recover "for a very long time." His own panzers would drive to the Volga just north of Stalingrad while Hoth's Fourth Panzer Army, pushing up from the southwest, would hit the river just south of the city. With Stalingrad thus caught in a vise of armor, the infantry would then attack head-on. It was a conventional plan, but such was the strength of his forces that Paulus thought the city might well be his in no more than a week.

At dawn on Sunday, August 23, the 16th Panzer Division launched the attack from a bridgehead about twenty-five miles north of Kalach. The steppe east of the Don was ideal terrain for armor—flat and baked hard by two rainless months—and these panzer men from Westphalia rolled ahead confidently under a canopy of Stuka dive bombers that occasionally dipped low to salute them with the piercing scream of their sirens. In the command vehicle of the signal corps company, barking out orders, rode Lieut. General Hans Hube, whom the troops referred to proudly as *Der Mensch*—"The Man." With the left sleeve of his tunic hanging limply—the result of a wound in the First World War—Hube was the only one-armed general in the German army, and a superb leader.

Hube's columns knifed through meager opposition. The Soviets tried to make a stand at an ancient defensive barrier called the Tatar Ditch, but the panzers easily smashed through its high earthen walls. As the armor raced on, new tactics were employed to deal with the pockets of resistance bypassed by the panzers. German reconnaissance planes spotted these

A wrecked Soviet rocket launcher and other equipment litter a plain near Kalach on the west bank of the Don after a fight for a vital bridgehead in late July. The Sixth Army's victory at Kalach was a steppingstone to Stalingrad.

Soviet concentrations and alerted special combat groups that peeled off from the main columns to eliminate them.

Progress was so rapid that Stalingrad soon loomed into view. Early that afternoon, sounding like a tour guide, the commander in the lead tank called out over his throat microphone: "Over on the right, the skyline of Stalingrad." And like tourists, tank commanders popped their heads through the turrets to see the silhouette of the city, from the onion-domed spires of the cathedrals in the old town in the south to the smokestacks of the modern factory district in the north. Here in 1918, when the city was known as Tsaritsyn, Stalin had participated in the Bolshevik military victory that he considered the turning point of the Revolution. Now an industrial city of 500,000, manufacturing more than one-fourth of the Soviet Union's tanks and other armored vehicles, Stalingrad stretched like a narrow ribbon for some thirty miles along the west bank of the Volga.

As Hube's vanguard headed for the northern suburbs, the lead panzers suddenly came under fire from artillery batteries on the outskirts of the city. The shelling was wildly inaccurate, and as the Germans knocked out the emplacements—thirty-seven in all—they discovered why: The gun crews consisted of civilians, women factory workers pressed hastily into service. Now they lay broken and maimed in their cotton dresses, counted among the first victims of the battle for Stalingrad.

About six o'clock in the evening, the first German vehicles rumbled through the northern suburb of Rynok and reached their destination, the Volga. Like Lieutenant Hans Oettl, a young officer from Munich who had carried his pet goat, Maedi, across the steppe in his armored vehicle, many

FW 189A-2 "Uhu"

A sword and a white eagle clutching yellow lightning bolts adorn the engine cowling of this FW 189, whose coded markings indicate that it belonged to the 1st Squadron of Tactical Reconnaissance Wing 31, which operated on the eastern front in the summer of 1942.

The Wehrmacht's Flying Eye

At first, traditionalists in the German air ministry scorned the concept of a tactical reconnaissance plane with two engines and twin tail booms as unworkable, predicting that it would produce an overweight and unstable aircraft. But by 1942, the unorthodox Focke Wulf 189 had become the Wehrmacht's "flying eye" on the eastern front.

The scout plane's sixty-foot wingspan was intersected by a pair of 465-horsepower Argus engines and a tapered nacelle that housed a crew of three. The cabin's glazed nose and a camera located behind the pilot's seat enabled the crew to scan the territory below much like the plane's keen-eyed namesake, the *Uhu*, or eagle owl.

The FW 189 had a top speed of 217 miles per hour, a range of just over 400 miles, and a maximum altitude of 23,000 feet. It was maneuverable enough to elude most Soviet fighters, and when attacked, its talons were sharp: The pilot operated a pair of forward-firing 7.9-mm machine guns installed in the wings while the navigator and flight mechanic protected the rear with two twin 7.9-mm machine guns—one pair mounted above and behind the pilot, the other pair in a revolving turret at the rear of the central nacelle.

of the Germans celebrated by climbing down the steep cliff to bathe in the river. Others followed trolley cars through the streets of Rynok, laughing uproariously at the panic of the passengers who looked back on this quiet Sunday evening to find German troops in the trucks behind them.

Hunkering down for the night in a hedgehog defense near the river, Hube's troops were treated to an awesome display of air power. Mounting its heaviest raid since the first day of the invasion, the Luftwaffe sent more than 600 planes against Stalingrad. Over half of the bombs dropped were incendiaries, and nearly every wooden structure in the city burned in a sea of flames so intense that German soldiers on the Don, forty miles in the rear, could read a newspaper by their light. Nearly 40,000 persons died in the raid, which was baldly designed to terrorize the city's inhabitants. The commander of Luftflotte 4, General Wolfram von Richthofen, cousin of the World War I ace, wrote in his diary that night: "We simply paralyzed the Russians."

After this spectacular beginning, the offensive sputtered and stalled. Hube's panzers attacked southward from Rynok into the industrial suburb of Spartakovka and ran up against trenches, pillboxes, and other fortifications defended by troops of the Soviet Sixty-Second Army and by men and women from the workers' militia. While the German assault staggered under an onslaught of fire, the Russians launched stinging counterattacks. In the forefront were T-34 tanks so fresh off the assembly line that many were still unpainted and driven by the workers who had just put them together at the Dzerzhinski tractor factory a few miles farther south.

Hube could expect no immediate help. His dash to the Volga had outdistanced the rest of the Sixth Army, even his comrades of the XIV Panzer Corps. Two divisions of motorized infantry, the 3d and 60th, were strung out behind him in a narrow corridor stretching back nearly to the Don. Gaps up to a dozen miles long separated the divisions, and Soviet counterattacks from the north poured into the spaces. Hube's division, stranded without reinforcements or resupply, was in such perilous straits after four days that the general briefly considered disobeying Hitler's orders and breaking out westward.

Not until August 30, a week after the lightning thrust to the Volga, did the pressure begin to ease. The motorized infantry closed up to seal off the corridor against attacks from the north and push supplies forward. The southern edge of the corridor was now covered by two divisions of infantry from the LI Corps. But the pivotal German thrust—and the most threatening one to Stalingrad's defenders—was developing south of the city, from Hoth's Fourth Panzer Army.

By the first week of August, Paulus's Sixth Army reached the Don River east of Stalingrad, and on August 7, a pincers movement by the XIV and XXIV Panzer Corps trapped the last Soviet forces still holding out on the west bank of the river, opposite Kalach. Over the next two weeks the Sixth Army consolidated its position and threw up bridgeheads over the river in preparation for the final drive on Stalingrad. The advance resumed on August 23 when the XIV Panzer Corps reached the Volga north of the city, while the LI Corps moved up on its right flank. To the south, meanwhile, Hoth's Fourth Panzer Army had closed to less than twenty miles from the city by the third week of August before it was stalled by stiffening enemy resistance. Anxious to effect a quick linkup with the Sixth Army, Hoth pulled his forces back and sent them on a long end run around to the west. On August 30, the XLVIII Panzer Corps swept through Gavrilovka and made contact with the LI Corps four days later. Both armies then slugged their way into Stalingrad.

Closing In on Stalin's City

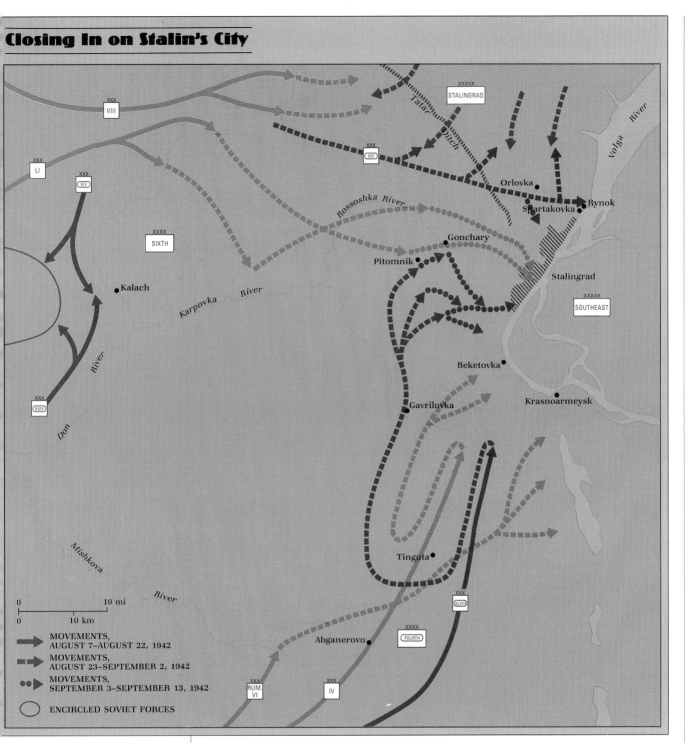

This had not been a happy time for Papa Hoth. His army, so powerful earlier in the summer, had been diverted south across the Don for the Caucasus campaign and then recalled for the drive against Stalingrad minus one of its two panzer corps. By August 20, Hoth found his army stalled north of Tinguta, a town twenty-five miles south of the city. His forward elements probed to within nine miles of Krasnoarmeysk, a river town commanding high ground south of Stalingrad on the bend in the Volga. But they were up against a line of heavily fortified hills, the southern cornerstone in the city's inner defense ring. For an entire week, during which time Hube's armor raced to the Volga up north, Hoth's panzers hammered away without success at the ravines, blockhouses, and tank-supported artillery and infantry of the Soviet Sixty-Fourth Army. Hoth lost two regimental commanders, thousands of other men, too many tanks—but not his cool sense of purpose. "We've got to tackle this thing differently," he told his chief of staff. "That's no ground for armor. We must regroup and mount our attack somewhere else, somewhere a long way from here."

Hoth began a daring sideslip that night. He quietly pulled his tanks and other mobile formations out of the line and replaced them with infantry to conceal his intentions. That night and the next, he wheeled the armored units past the rear of his infantry on the left and reassembled them thirty miles to the south and west. From this new position, he could outflank those "damned hills" south of the city that had been bleeding his army.

Hoth struck northward on August 29. His gambit stunned the enemy. Outflanked Soviet divisions retreated in confusion. The next morning, Hoth's motorized infantry intercepted thousands of Russian soldiers wandering the steppe. During the next two days, Hoth's advance units pierced the inner belt of defenses at Gavrilovka and reached the railway to Stalingrad, less than twenty miles west of the city.

Their sudden success created an extraordinary opportunity. If Paulus could turn the mobile formations of the Sixth Army southward to meet Hoth's panzers, thousands of enemy troops would be cut off before they could retreat into the city. The joint German columns then might be able to storm Stalingrad virtually unopposed. Messages from Army Group B ordering the southward thrust went out to Paulus on August 30 as soon as Hoth gained Gavrilovka and again the following day. Paulus hesitated, afraid to strip his left flank, where the XIV Panzer Corps still had to fend off attacks from the north. When Paulus's infantry finally joined up with Hoth's panzers at Gonchary on September 3, they were only a few miles from the center of Stalingrad. They arrived two days too late to trap the enemy, however, who had retreated from the open steppe into the streets of the city, where mobile tactics would no longer prevail.

During the following week, the Germans tightened their grip on the city. Although the XIV Panzer Corps was too preoccupied with attacks from the north to progress against the industrial district in the northern section of

On August 23, a column of trucks and half-tracks of the 16th Panzer Division rumbles east toward the Volga River past a burning Russian truck. A bloodied courier (*inset*) reports on stiff Soviet resistance ahead.

the city, Paulus's infantry pressed up against the western fringes of central Stalingrad. Once again, however, Hoth's panzers and motorized infantry delivered the most telling blow. Skirting along the southern edge of the city eastward and then north, the Fourth Panzer Army slashed to the Volga. Hoth's men then seized the objectives they had vainly sought before his daring gambit—the hilly southern suburbs of Krasnoarme and Kuperosnoye. By doing so, they split off the Soviet Sixty-Fourth Army below Stalingrad, leaving the Sixty-Second Army alone within the city.

Paulus now confronted a defense perimeter shrunken nearly to the limits of the city itself: a few miles deep and twenty miles long between the north and south suburbs. It was defended by that single battered Soviet army, the Sixty-Second, with 50,000 troops and 100 or so tanks. Against the central and southern sectors of this perimeter, Paulus was preparing to hurl 100,000 men and 500 tanks, supported by more than 1,000 aircraft.

The two-pronged offensive began on Sunday morning, September 13, after a punishing bombardment by Stukas and artillery. While Hoth's four

As the 24th Panzer Division rushes north to Stalingrad, an officer scans the horizon for signs of the enemy. One German wrote,

"To take Stalingrad is not so difficult for us. The Führer knows where the Russians' weak point is. Victory is not far away."

German troops ascend Hill 102, a strategic prize with a commanding view of Stalingrad's northern and central suburbs (*background*). The rough terrain around the city hindered the advancing German army. "From the wide expanses of the steppe land," a German general recorded, "the war moved into the jagged gullies of the Volga hills, spread out over uneven, pitted, rugged country."

divisions struck from the south, three infantry divisions pushed in from the west. Their assaults were separated by an impassable east-west barrier, the 200-foot-deep gorge carved by the Tsaritsa River, which cut off the southern third of the city. The infantry columns north of the gorge aimed for the downtown government buildings and the main railway station. On the left, they headed for Mamayev Hill, a 335-foot eminence that dominated the center of the city. Dubbed Hill 102 on the military maps for its height in meters above sea level, it was actually a kurgan, or ancient burial ground, that now served as a popular picnic area. By nightfall, German infantry swarmed in the woods only a mile west of the hill.

On Monday, the Germans broke into the city streets on both sides of the gorge. To the south, elements of the 24th Panzer Division captured the southern railway station and stormed toward the Volga. To the north, tanks and foot soldiers by the truckload burst into the heart of the city. They took the crest of Mamayev Hill and seized the main rail station and parts of nearby Red Square *(see map, page 85)*.

Troops from the 71st Infantry Division, fighting their way a block at a time through downtown, cut a narrow corridor eastward to the river. Their goal was the central ferry landing, the main crossing point for Russian supplies and reinforcements from the east bank of the Volga. The Germans came within a half-mile of the landing at dusk. But depleted by heavy casualties— one battalion had only fifty able-bodied men left—they were held off by a small NKVD unit who formed a skirmish line around the landing and were resupplied by a motorboat just as they ran out of ammunition. The importance of the central landing was dramatized that night when 10,000 reinforcements from a crack Soviet unit, the 13th Guards Division, were ferried into battle from the east bank. These troops were the forerunners of nearly 100,000 Russian soldiers who would cross the Volga during the next two weeks in a desperate attempt to stave off the Germans.

The pace of the German attack slackened. Once ground was taken it had to be fought for over and over again. By September 16, the main railway station had changed hands fifteen times. Contenders for the summit of Mamayev Hill stormed up and down the slopes. Any street, as a German officer wrote home, was "measured no longer by meters but by corpses."

This was a new kind of combat for the Germans, who referred to it as *Rattenkrieg*, or war of the rats. Their superiority in the air and in armor that had proved so devastating in the open field no longer guaranteed success. The Luftwaffe flew an average of 1,000 sorties a day, but the pilots found it impossible to pinpoint a target when forces on the ground were engaged at arm's length. Panzers could blow away buildings, but squads of Soviet defenders survived in the cellars. The panzers bogged down in the narrow, rubble-strewn streets, their thinly protected rear decks falling prey to Russian artillery, hand-held antitank rifles, and even grenades tossed from second-story windows.

Day and night, hundreds of miniature battles raged in the fire-blackened heart of the city. The savage fighting flared from floor to floor and room to room within a building, and was fought to the finish in the most primitive fashion with knives, clubs, sharpened shovels, and even stones.

"My God, why have you forsaken us?" wrote a lieutenant of the 24th Panzer Division during that terrible autumn of 1942. "We have fought fifteen days for a single house, with mortars, grenades, machine guns, and bayonets. Already by the third day, fifty-four German corpses are strewn in the cellars, on the landings, and on the staircases. The front is a corridor between burnt-out rooms; it is the thin ceiling between two floors."

In their rush toward the Volga, the Germans left behind islands of resistance that took days or weeks to eliminate. One Soviet bastion was a wheat-filled grain elevator on the southern edge of the city. The struggle for this enormous concrete edifice, which was defended at the start by fewer than fifty Russians, began on the second day of the German offensive, September 14. "The battalion is suffering heavy losses," wrote a German soldier, Wilhelm Hoffmann. "There are no more than sixty men left in each company. The elevator is occupied not by men but by devils that no flames or bullets can destroy." After the garrison was reinforced by a platoon of Russian marines, Hoffmann wrote in despair: "If all the buildings of Stalingrad are defended like this, then none of our soldiers will get back to Germany." It was September 22 before the defenders were cleared out of the smoke and stench of the smoldering grain, and the job ultimately required elements of three of Hoth's divisions.

Slowly the invaders wiped out the nests of fiercest resistance. By September 27, two weeks after Paulus launched his offensive, he could claim conquest of at least half of the city. Hoth's panzers—now under Paulus's command—held the old city south of the Tsaritsa River. Paulus's own infantry occupied the central city, even the vital ferry landing, which had been taken on September 25. But Paulus had no cause for celebration. The past six weeks of fighting, from the Don to the Volga, had cost the Sixth Army 10 percent of its troops: 7,700 dead, 31,000 wounded. Soviet casualties, not counting thousands of desertions, were twice that. And the key to Stalingrad, its industrial northern district, was still to be conquered.

On that Sunday, September 27, the focus of the fighting shifted northward. The objectives were the four major factories—together with the settlements housing their workers—that occupied a broad strip nearly a dozen

During the fall of 1942, Paulus' Sixth Army and Hoth's Fourth Panzer Army engaged General Vasily Chuikov's Sixty-Second Army in a costly yard-by-yard struggle for Stalingrad. By mid-September, the Germans controlled most of the central and southern parts of the city, but it was early October before the swastika flew securely over Red Square. Now the Sixth Army engaged in a bitter fight for the shattered industrial complexes in Stalingrad's northern sector. By early November, the German forces controlled almost the entire city. But the Soviet defenders, supplied by ferries running across the Volga, managed to cling tenaciously to a handful of bridgeheads on the river's west bank, while to the south and northwest the Red Army stood poised to encircle and destroy the besiegers.

A Battle among the Ruins

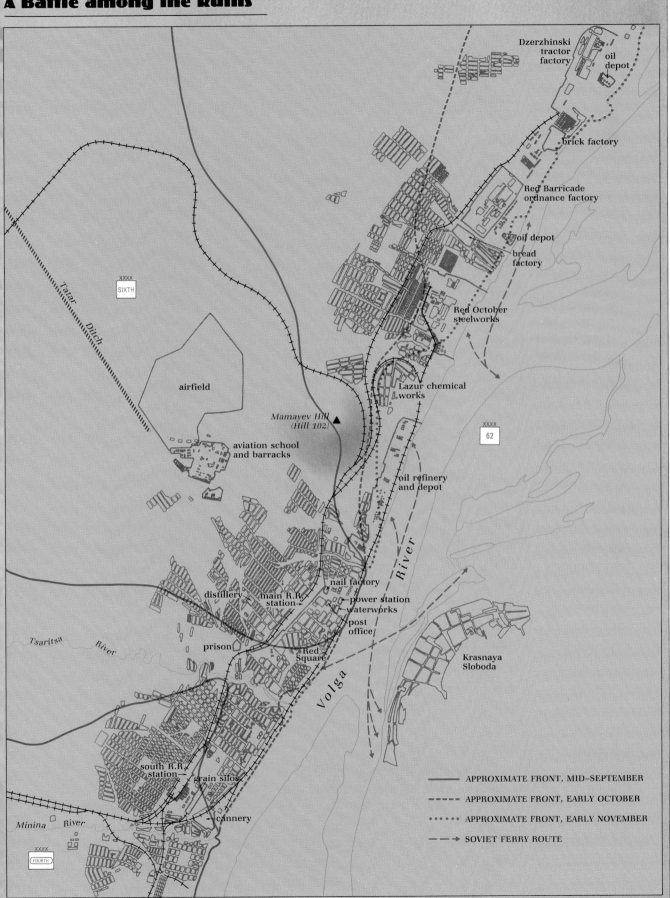

Dzerzhinski
tractor
factory

oil
depot

brick factory

Red Barricade
ordnance factory

oil depot

bread
factory

Red October
steelworks

XXXX
SIXTH

Tatar Ditch

airfield

Lazur chemical
works

Mamayev Hill
(Hill 102)

aviation school
and barracks

XXXX
62

oil refinery
and depot

River

nail factory

distillery

main R.R.
station

power station

waterworks

post
office

Tsaritsa River

prison

Red
Square

Krasnaya
Sloboda

Volga

south R.R.
station

grain silos

cannery

Minina River

XXXX
FOURTH

―――――― APPROXIMATE FRONT, MID–SEPTEMBER

- - - - - - APPROXIMATE FRONT, EARLY OCTOBER

· · · · · · · · APPROXIMATE FRONT, EARLY NOVEMBER

– – –► SOVIET FERRY ROUTE

miles long abutting the Volga. From the north, these were the tank-producing Dzerzhinski tractor factory, the Red Barricade ordnance factory, the Red October steelworks, which manufactured small arms, and the Lazur chemical works.

Paulus regrouped his divisions and closed in on the factories from the north, west, and south. The 71st Infantry Division, marching north along the Volga from downtown, was reminded by the bedlam on its left that pockets of resistance still remained in the old sector. In the center of the city, Germans and Russians continued to fight for control of Mamayev Hill.

Before Paulus mounted a full-scale attack on the factory district from the north and west, he wanted to eliminate an enemy salient near the town of Orlovka, three miles west of the tractor factory. Soviet forces outside the German corridor had created this bulge by pushing down from the north against the corridor held by the XIV Panzer Corps. Some five miles long and two miles deep, it threatened the flanks of Sixth Army's assault columns. On September 29, Paulus attacked the Orlovka salient with regiments from four different divisions.

Among the units committed from the 60th Motorized Division was a company led by Lieutenant Heinrich Klotz. At the age of forty-three, Klotz commanded the oldest group of Germans on the battlefield, one-third of whom, like Klotz, had fought in the Great War. Klotz and his veterans were growing weary of the struggle for Stalingrad. He complained bitterly when told there would be no tanks available to support his company's assault. Sensing disaster that morning, he nevertheless dutifully signaled with his arm and led his men up a hill. Soviet planes suddenly appeared overhead and swept down to bomb and strafe. The Germans would succeed in pinching off the salient a couple of days later, but when Klotz went out with the medics to collect the casualties that first night, he discovered that 90 of the 120 men he had led into battle now lay dead or wounded.

Paulus, too, was growing sick at heart even as he prepared for what he hoped would be the final offensive. Dredging up the last of his reserves from back at the Don, he now had eleven divisions in and around Stalingrad, maintaining his two-to-one superiority over the defenders. But the pronounced nervous tic on the left side of his face betrayed his anxiety that these numbers were not enough. "Without reinforcements," his own chief of staff reported, "the army is not going to take Stalingrad very soon." Turning back was out of the question. General Zeitzler, Halder's successor, surprised Hitler by advocating a withdrawal. But the Führer, speaking in Berlin on September 30, vowed to take the city and then assured his audience, "You can be certain no one will get us away from there."

During October, the struggle for northern Stalingrad alternated between withering blasts of massed firepower and grueling small-unit combat. On October 2, for example, German artillery zeroed in on the Red October steelworks. Enormous oil tanks went up in a blast that shook the city; fiery waves of flaming fuel crashed down the cliff into the Volga. Three days later, Stukas flew more than 2,000 sorties against the factory district—700 against the Dzerzhinski tractor factory alone. On that same October 5, more than 300 Soviet guns and mortars on the east bank of the Volga fired on the Germans for forty minutes nonstop.

Meanwhile, the crack of the sniper's bullet resounded amid the rubble. Russian snipers, perching in the skeletal remains of ruined buildings, took a fearful toll of the German infantry. One sharpshooter, Vasily Zaitsev, a former shepherd who had honed his skills hunting deer in the foothills of the Ural Mountains, became a national hero. He arrived in Stalingrad on September 20 and in ten days was credited with killing forty Germans. Zaitsev then began training apprentices in his deadly art at a school established at the Lazur chemical works.

To counter the likes of Zaitsev, the Germans brought in their own expert, SS Colonel Heinz Thorwald, who directed a snipers' school near Berlin. Thorwald, stalking the no man's land between the factories and Mamayev Hill, soon found the mark against two of Zaitsev's most experienced colleagues. Then, in a nerve-racking hunt conducted through the telescopic sights on their rifles, the two master snipers began stalking each other. Before dawn, the adversaries found cover in the rubble and lay there all day, scanning the ruins before them in search of their quarry. Occasionally, one would wave a helmet or glove, attempting to trick the other into firing and thus disclosing his position.

On the third day, Thorwald struck. He was lying in ambush beneath a sheet of iron when he saw someone carelessly rise up above a parapet. It was a companion of Zaitsev, and Thorwald shot him in the shoulder. But Zaitsev now knew where the German was hiding. The next day, Zaitsev went into position with another companion and a plan. The man slowly raised his helmet. Thorwald fired. The man screamed as if shot. When Thorwald lifted his head slightly for a better look, Zaitsev was waiting. He shot the German between the eyes. By Russian count, Zaitsev claimed 242 German lives during the battle of Stalingrad—only to lose his sharpshooter's vision when a land mine went off and blinded him.

On October 14, Paulus mounted his biggest offensive against northern Stalingrad. Massing three infantry divisions and 200 tanks from two panzer divisions, he smashed into the milelong complex of shops and assembly lines at the tractor works. The bombing, shelling, and small-arms fire was so intense that the smoke and the dust created by crumbling walls blotted out the sun and blanketed the area so densely that the combatants could see scarcely more than a half-dozen yards. With the panzers and Stukas blasting Soviet strongpoints, the Germans seized most of the plant. That night, they pushed through to the Volga on a front more than a mile wide, splitting the Soviet Sixty-Second Army in two. The assault units turned south and fought their way into both the Red Barricade ordnance factory and the Red October steelworks. Russian losses during the first three days of the new offensive amounted to 13,000 killed and wounded, nearly one-fourth of the shrinking forces inside the city.

Inside the Red Barricade complex, the offensive slowed. It was October 24 before tank-supported motorcyclists from the 14th Panzer Division finally took their first building, a bread factory at the southern corner of the complex. The assault on the second building bogged down the following day. A sergeant named Esser crouched behind a wrecked armored car and surveyed the carnage. Across the road lay the body of his company com-

Russian soldiers dart for cover through the charred ruins of a workers' settlement in southern Stalingrad. German officers conceded that the Russians were superior in the building-to-building combat that characterized the struggle for Stalingrad.

Germans manning a howitzer in the southern part of Stalingrad take aim through smoldering rubble at targets in the distance. The grain elevator (*background, center*) was the scene of some of the bloodiest fighting in the city.

mander. Behind him was the platoon commander—also dead. A squad leader lay nearby, wounded in the head and groaning in delirium.

It was all too much for Esser. Like a man gone berserk, he jumped to his feet, screamed "Forward!" and led a dozen of his platoon's survivors across sixty yards of open courtyard to the second building. Reaching the wall unscathed, they blasted a hole in it with explosives, crept through, and caught the Russian defenders crouching by the windows firing into the courtyard. Esser and his men mowed them down with machine pistols and then surprised the Russians on the second floor. The little band did not rest until it had taken eighty prisoners, captured an antitank gun and sixteen heavy machine guns, and seized control of the entire building.

The offensive, which lasted fifteen days, left both sides limp and exhausted—and the Germans in control of 90 percent of the city. Except for the scores of little spots of resistance that flared up periodically like glowing embers in the ruins, the Soviets managed to cling to only two patches of ground, containing a few factory buildings and a few miles of riverbank. One of their two separate bridgeheads embraced parts of the northern suburbs of Rynok and Spartakovka; the other took in the Lazur chemical works and parts of the Red October steelworks. In the latter area, the Russian commander, Vasily Chuikov, had been forced to move his headquarters again, this time to a tunnel carved out of a sandstone cliff overlooking the river. It was his fifth command post in seven weeks, and Chuikov, like Paulus with his facial tic, was showing the strain: He was so badly afflicted with nervous eczema that he had to wear bandages to cover the open sores on his hands.

Conquering the remaining 10 percent of the city offered no strategic advantage to Hitler but had great psychological significance for him. Stalingrad had become a symbol of the stubborn Soviet spirit, and Hitler badly needed a victory. By early November, his drive into the Caucasus had stalled, and in the north, Manstein's Eleventh Army had failed to break the stalemate around Leningrad. The news from North Africa was also bad. Rommel was retreating westward out of Egypt after a major British victory at El Alamein. And when Hitler arrived in Munich on November 8 to celebrate the nineteenth anniversary of the Beer Hall Putsch, he was greeted with reports of the American and British landings in Morocco and Tunisia.

Hitler's frustration had been evident the previous night as his special train stopped at a siding en route to the Bavarian capital. The Führer was seated with guests at dinner in his elegant dining car when he noticed that a freight train had pulled up on an adjacent track. It was laden with bedraggled soldiers—some of them wounded—from the eastern front. One of Hitler's dinner companions, Albert Speer, minister of armaments and war production, later noted that the Führer once would have made a point of showing himself at the window on such an occasion. But when he saw these veterans staring at him from just a few feet away, Hitler made no gesture of greeting. Instead, he ordered a servant to pull down the shades.

To make good his reaffirmation at Munich—"No power on earth will force us out of Stalingrad again!"—Hitler ordered up reinforcements. These were not the infantry divisions that Paulus pleaded for but five elite bat-

In October 1942, a swastika proclaims a fleeting Nazi victory from the shell of the Univermag department store, a building whose basement later served as headquarters for the commander of Germany's Sixth Army. After weeks of furious combat in the city, a spent German soldier (*opposite*), indifferent to the fire raging behind him, stares at the world with lifeless eyes.

talions of combat engineers. They were specialists in blasting their way through obstacles with flamethrowers and explosives, and Paulus put them to work immediately.

On the morning of November 11, the engineers fought through the ghastly wreckage of the Red Barricade ordnance factory and into the area just east of it. One of their objectives, the Commissar's House, a large brick structure that commanded the local terrain, was bristling with defenders firing out from tiny peepholes with lethal accuracy. Sappers of the 50th Battalion broke into the building and chased the Russians into the cellars. In their frenzy to get at them, the Germans ripped up the floor. They tossed down cans of gasoline and set them afire and then lowered satchel charges of dynamite and detonated them. Just in case any of the enemy were still alive, they laid down smoke cartridges to blind them.

Such actions cost the engineers dearly. During their first fierce days in Stalingrad, one-third of the 3,000-man force fell dead or wounded. But the infusion of fresh skills and a final lunge from the battle-weary infantry enabled the Germans to push back the defenses and slash another path to the Volga. Paulus now had the enemy divided into three precarious toeholds on the river's west bank: the ground held by the main force south of the steelworks, a wedge only 100 yards deep near the ordnance factory, and a patch of land north of the tractor factory in Rynok. There, at Rynok, the 16th Panzer Division fought in the November cold for the very ground it had seized nearly three months before in that first thrilling dash to the Volga on a hot Sunday in August.

If Paulus no longer could muster strength for one more major push, he hoped at least that the onset of winter might finish off the enemy. Packs of ice were building up in the Volga, making it impassable to the small ferries and barges that brought reinforcements and supplies to the embattled west bank. It would likely be several weeks before the river froze solid and allowed men and vehicles to cross on the ice. On November 18, the temperature dropped below freezing again, and the Russian defenders—cold, hungry, and growing short of ammunition—spent their fourth straight day without the arrival of supply boats.

During that wintry afternoon, as the Germans renewed the struggle in scores of savage little fights, ominous messages for Paulus were pouring in. For weeks, the Rumanians guarding the German flanks south of Stalingrad on the Volga and northwest of the city near the Don had warned of massive Red Army buildups in front of them. Now these sectors buzzed with reports of long columns of Soviet infantry assembling and hundreds of Soviet tanks revving their engines. In a startling reversal of roles, the intrepid invaders of Stalingrad were about to become the tragic defenders. ✚

German soldiers near the enemy lines spread a flag to warn the Luftwaffe of their unit's position.

An Aerial Fist for the Army

Throughout the summer offensive of 1942, the Luftwaffe, as in previous campaigns, functioned as the aerial fist of the German army. With the exception of a few attacks against Soviet oil installations and logistical lifelines, Luftflotte 4, or Air Fleet 4, devoted itself to clearing the way for Army Group South's surge toward Stalingrad and the Caucasus. Air-liaison officers rode in the vanguard of the motorized spearheads to coordinate air-to-ground operations from the front lines.

"Having no strategic mission of its own," explained an aviator, "the Luftwaffe gradually became nothing but a supporting arm of the ground forces, used more or less as long-range artillery." Indeed, the army, with too few men and tanks, was in constant need of air support to smash enemy resistance and to probe ahead of the broadening front.

Thanks in part to this interservice cooperation, the Germans by the end of August had reached the gates of Stalingrad and had planted their flag on Mount Elbrus, the highest peak in the Caucasus. However, like its partners on the ground, the Luftwaffe was losing the war of matériel; before winter set in, control of the skies—at least in terms of sheer numbers of aircraft—was passing to the Soviets.

Reconnoitering Boundless Russia

Every day, German tactical reconnaissance planes took to the skies to reconnoiter the vast and unfamiliar Russian landscape that swallowed up the invaders as they pushed eastward.

Often the pilots brought back photographs revealing features that were not on German maps, and field commanders used the information to make last-minute changes in their attack plans that saved both time and lives. At the Laba River in the Caucasus, for example, the 16th Motorized Infantry Division stalled because no one could find a way across. "Then," recalled a soldier, "we received the latest aerial photographs and there was a surprise. The photographs showed a new railroad bridge that did not appear on the map." German motorized units soon were pouring across the newfound bridge.

General Wolfram von Richthofen, commander of Luftflotte 4, studies the defenses of Stalingrad through field glasses on August 23, 1942. In the half-track just behind him is General Hans Hube, whose 16th Panzer Division reached the Volga that day.

An FW 189A scouts along a winding river in the Caucasus. Small but rugged, well-armed and maneuverable, the Focke Wulf was a tough target for Soviet fighters to hit.

New Missions for a Versatile Old Bomber

Because the Soviet fighter command was relatively weak, Germany's aging twin-engine Heinkel bomber enjoyed a second life on the eastern front. The Germans used the lumbering old He 111s for jobs never dreamed of by the designers who created the plane in the early 1930s. The new missions included flying air cover for advancing troops *(right)*, providing close ground support, airlifting supplies and personnel, even towing cargo-laden gliders—all this in addition to carrying out the Heinkel's traditional bombing runs against rail junctions and concentrations of troops and supplies.

He 111s fly protective cover for an advancing column of motorized infantry. Shot down in droves during the Battle of Britain, the bomber became a welcome sight to German ground forces in Russia.

Bombed out by German Stukas, Russian T-34 tanks litter the battlefield near the city of Kharkov.

A Stuka flies above smoke from Soviet antiaircraft shells. Often having no radio contact with the dive bombers, German ground spotters directed their fire with flare pistols and markers.

A swarm of Ju 87s streak away after unloading their bombs on targets near the Don River. When possible, the Stuka pilots tried to dive on Russian tanks from the rear, where they were most vulnerable.

Stukas: The Best Tank Busters

The Junkers 87 dive bomber (the Stuka) supported German ground troops in Russia, just as it had in the blitzkrieg triumphs over Poland, Holland, Belgium, and France. The ungainly, gull-wing Stuka was especially devastating at breaking up attacks by Soviet tanks.

"Only a miracle could save us from utter catastrophe," recalled a German soldier whose unit was on the point of being overrun by enemy armor. "And the miracle happened. Suddenly, the skies were filled with a mutter that grew into a roar. We looked up and saw wave upon wave of Stukas bearing down in wedge formation. They dipped their right wings sharply and, with a nerve-shattering screech of their sirens, came down on the tanks. Mushrooms of smoke uncoiled into the sky, and the wall of metal dissolved in panic."

The loser in a dogfight, a burning Russian Il 2 attack plane *(above)* hurtles toward the ground while its pilot parachutes into captivity *(right)*. The pilot *(opposite, far right)* was interrogated later by German fliers, including the man who shot him down, Group Commander Gordon Gollob *(wearing the Knight's Cross)*. Gollob, born in Vienna, became one of the Luftwaffe's leading aces; during two weeks of concentrated air combat over the Caucasus in August of 1942, he destroyed thirty-two enemy planes.

Masters of the Soviet Skies

By the third year of the war, Luftwaffe fighter wings were rarely operating at full strength. Their planes were superior to the Russians', however, and the well-trained German pilots had little difficulty keeping enemy fighters off the backs of German ground-support aircraft.

Because the German fighters were spread so thin, their activities were restricted to the most critical sectors. As one pilot explained,

"Aviation fuel and ammunition were so scarce that we were forced to operate as small tactical units over limited areas of the front."

Despite these constraints, the Luftwaffe ran up some amazing scores. During a three-day stretch in July 1942, while supporting the eastward drives of the Sixth and Second armies, German pilots shot down ninety-two Soviet planes and set another thirty-five on fire.

Masters of the Soviet Skies

By the third year of the war, Luftwaffe fighter wings were rarely operating at full strength. Their planes were superior to the Russians', however, and the well-trained German pilots had little difficulty keeping enemy fighters off the backs of German ground-support aircraft.

Because the German fighters were spread so thin, their activities were restricted to the most critical sectors. As one pilot explained,

"Aviation fuel and ammunition were so scarce that we were forced to operate as small tactical units over limited areas of the front."

Despite these constraints, the Luftwaffe ran up some amazing scores. During a three-day stretch in July 1942, while supporting the eastward drives of the Sixth and Second armies, German pilots shot down ninety-two Soviet planes and set another thirty-five on fire.

Laying Waste to Stalingrad

In early September, the Luftwaffe launched a methodical bombing assault on Stalingrad to soften up the city for the ground attack to come. The bombers' primary targets were airfields and factories, railroad installations, and the boats that ferried reinforcements and supplies across the Volga.

The bombing required pinpoint accuracy because the vanguard of the German army had almost reached the enemy's positions. Luftwaffe tacticians used aerial photographs to identify specific targets, then issued marked maps to the pilots before takeoff.

The pounding from the air contributed mightily to reducing Stalingrad to a heap of rubble, but it failed to dislodge the Russians. "The more ruins we created," conceded one general, "the more cover the defenders were able to find."

A formation of Stukas crosses the Volga River in search of targets. Although the German planes faced little opposition from enemy aircraft, anti-aircraft fire was intense.

A bomb plummets toward the city center. The eyelet-shaped line on the ground is the Lazur chemical works' railway siding, a popular target that German pilots referred to as "the tennis racket."

Factories in Stalingrad's industrial complex go up in smoke after a strike by German dive bombers. The wooden buildings still intact in the foreground are workers' housing.

THREE

The Cauldron on the Volga

Dawn came slowly to the wintry steppe on the morning of November 19, 1942. A heavy snow during the night had given way to wispy fog, with the temperature hovering around twenty degrees. In his bunker, Sergeant Wolf Pelikan awoke to the rumble and tremor of distant artillery. A weather observer attached to a German outpost near the great bend in the Don River 100 miles northwest of Stalingrad, Pelikan was not greatly alarmed by the sound of the guns. There had been barrages before, but his sector was relatively quiet, far from the awful maelstrom of the city itself. Still, as the cannonade continued, Pelikan climbed from his cot and started putting on his uniform. When the firing abruptly ceased, he finished dressing in a more leisurely manner and started out the door, heading for breakfast.

Just then a company messenger dashed up, waving his arms and shouting, "The Ivans are here! The Ivans are here!"

"You're crazy!" Pelikan yelled back. But then he looked to the north, and as the wind blew away the mist, he saw a number of large, squat, menacing tanks crowning the crest of a small hill. They were Soviet T-34s. Pelikan froze, then gaped at another terrifying sight: hundreds of Rumanian troops running wildly toward him across the landscape. As they dodged through his outpost, the Rumanians screamed that the Russians were close behind.

At this, a terrible fright overcame the tiny German unit. The outpost's commanding officer ran to a light plane and took off, heading south. Pelikan and the other men grabbed what belongings they could and threw them into trucks. The drivers roared away, bumping and swerving across the rough, snow-covered terrain. Wedged into a bakery truck, Pelikan looked back and watched the Soviet tanks, still standing motionless on the slope, until the ominous sight vanished into the haze.

Similar scenes of terror and flight enveloped the northwestern rim of the huge salient the German Sixth Army had created in its thrust at Stalingrad. Intelligence had warned of a Soviet counterattack, and aerial reconnaissance had observed unmistakable signs of an enemy buildup. But when the stroke came, it was far swifter and more powerful than anyone had imag-

Searching for shelter from Russian snipers and the numbing cold at the end of 1942, German soldiers of the Sixth Army poke through a Stalingrad building that months of bombing and street-fighting had stripped of every comfort. "Animals flee this hell," wrote an officer trapped in the dying city. "Only men endure."

Attacking a front held by the Rumanian Third Army northwest of Stalingrad, Red Army infantrymen *(left)* in winter camouflage ride into battle atop T-34 tanks on November 19, 1942. The advancing Soviets knew that the Rumanians' morale was low and their desertion rate high.

Two German infantrymen, crouching in the snow behind a captured Soviet light antitank gun, fight in vain to maintain the flank abandoned by their fleeing Rumanian allies. Two years earlier, Hitler told his generals that the fate of German formations would never depend on the reliability of the Rumanians.

ined. The assault began with the tremendous artillery barrage Sergeant Pelikan had heard from eight miles away: 3,500 cannons and mortars blasting huge holes in the Axis defensive perimeter. After eighty minutes of bombardment, which commenced at 7:20 a.m., the Soviet Fifth Tank Army lunged forward from its bridgehead on the Don at Serafimovich—two armored corps with about 500 tanks each, a cavalry corps, and six infantry divisions. At the same moment, the Soviet Twenty-First Army, almost as strong, struck southward from its bridgehead at Kletskaya, twenty-five miles southeast of Serafimovich.

The tank phalanxes rumbled forward, firing as they advanced, only half visible in the gray mist. With them came masses of Russian infantrymen garbed in white winter camouflage, taking cover behind the tanks and clinging to the flanks of the machines. In all, about half a million Soviet troops, commanded by Major General Nikolay Vatutin, assailed the northern perimeter of the salient.

Both of these Soviet hammer blows fell on sectors held by divisions sent

107

to Russia by Germany's ally, Rumania. Although ill-trained and poorly equipped, a number of Rumanian units resisted fiercely for a time; others simply succumbed to what one German general called "an indescribable tank panic" and fled at the first sight of the oncoming T-34s. Within twenty-four hours, the Rumanian Third Army had disintegrated, leaving a colossal fifty-mile gap in the salient's northern perimeter. More than 75,000 men were either dead or had surrendered—and often to give up meant death. All along the front, Soviet soldiers fired indiscriminately into the ragged ranks of figures walking toward them with hands upraised.

As squadrons of Soviet T-34s roared out of the haze to hit supply dumps, communications centers, and headquarters detachments, many small German units positioned just behind the front joined Sergeant Pelikan in flight. Many commanders, without orders from General Friedrich Paulus's Sixth Army headquarters, led their men eastward toward the German-held crossing over the Don River, in the general direction of Stalingrad. They found themselves caught up in huge traffic jams on the roads. Shepherding his mortars toward the Don, Lieutenant Hermann Kästle watched in amazement as vicious fistfights broke out among the troops jockeying for position. Late that afternoon, as Kästle was about to cross a bridge over the Don, a panzer lieutenant appeared and at gunpoint ordered him to stand aside; his tank, the lieutenant spat, had higher priority.

One faint hope of slowing the Soviet onslaught rested with the XLVIII Panzer Corps of Lieut. General Ferdinand Heim. The heart of the corps was the 22d Panzer Division, but it was an organization sorely beset by circumstance. Stationed behind the Rumanians in a presumably static sector, the 22d had received no fuel for training or testing runs, and consequently had dug its tanks into pits and covered them with straw as protection against the cold. Now, when the crews tried to start the engines, they found that less than half would turn over. Mice, burrowing through the straw and into the idle vehicles, had nibbled away the insulation of the electrical wiring: Ignitions, battery feeds, turret sights, and guns were out of commission. Several tanks caught fire from short circuits when the drivers hit the starters. Instead of 104 tanks, the 22d ended up with only 42 capable of facing the Russians—and half of those were disabled by further mechanical failures and other problems as they hurried into combat.

Even so, when the depleted 22d encountered the Soviet spearhead on November 19, it conducted itself gallantly. Within minutes, twenty-six broken and blazing T-34s lay before the guns of the German division's tanks and *Panzerjäger*, or antitank, battalion. Had there been panzer units to cover the 22d's flanks, the Soviet thrust might have been halted, but there was nothing to the right or the left—except desperately fleeing Rumanians

On the morning of November 1 with most of the decimated German divisions of Army Grou B clustered around Stalingrad, the Russians sprang a carefully planned trap. Infantry and arm of the Twenty-First and Fifth Tank armies, surging out of bridgeheads along the Don around Serafimovich and Kletskaya, slammed into Army Group B's vulnerable northern flank, scattering the Rumanian Third Army and beating off counterattacks by the XLVIII Panzer Corps. The next day, the Soviets smashed through the equally vulnerable German flan south of Stalingrad. Both spearheads then raced to a rendezvous in the rear of Paulus's Sixth Army, bypassing German strongpoints and scarcely stopping to gather up prisoners. On November 23, the two Soviet juggernauts linked u at Sovetski, closing the ring on 250,000 Axis troops.

Sixth Army in the Bag

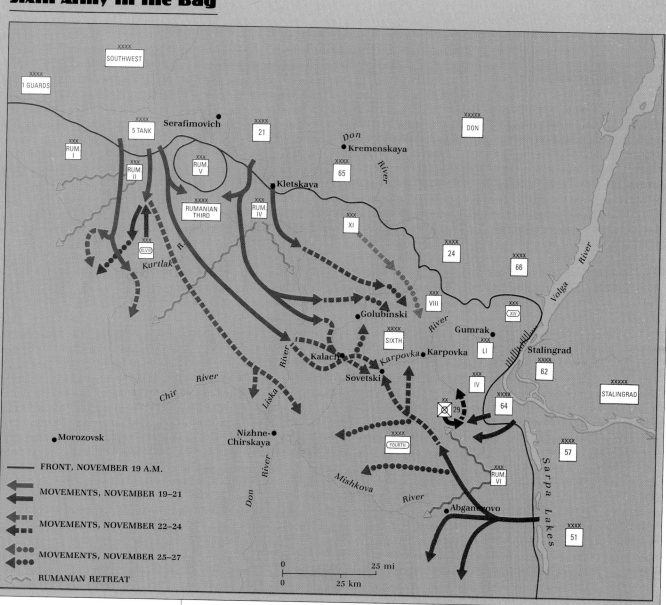

FRONT, NOVEMBER 19 A.M.

MOVEMENTS, NOVEMBER 19–21

MOVEMENTS, NOVEMBER 22–24

MOVEMENTS, NOVEMBER 25–27

RUMANIAN RETREAT

and more T-34s flowing past. It was clear to Heim that he faced envelopment and annihilation. The general broke contact and dodged away beyond the left bank of the Chir River.

It was a sound move. But instead of saluting his general for good sense, Hitler interpreted the action as cowardice. Heim was stripped of his rank and ordered back to Germany, where he was hauled before a drumhead court-martial at which Göring presided, and was clapped into prison.

By now the Soviets were unstoppable. On November 22, just four days into the offensive, the Fifth Tank Army stood on the banks of the Liska River, sixty miles from their starting point and only twenty-five miles from the bridge that carried the main German supply route across the Don at Kalach. That span fell intact to the Soviets the same afternoon, under yet another preposterous set of circumstances.

The bridge had been prepared for demolition, and a platoon of German engineers stood by for orders to blow it up. However, the Germans held a training school at Kalach that was using several captured Soviet tanks for

109

firing demonstrations, and the engineers at the bridge mistook the on-coming Soviet tanks and personnel carriers for the school's vehicles. Five tanks had charged onto the bridge before a sergeant grabbed his binoculars and hollered: "Those damn tanks are Russian!" An 88-mm gun opened up and knocked out two tanks. But it was too late. The rest of the T-34s kept going, while sixty Russians burst from the personnel carriers and killed most of the engineers. Before long, twenty-five Soviet tanks were on the east bank of the Don and fanning out to establish a bridgehead.

Ordinarily, the Germans might have looked to the skies for assistance, to the Stukas of their vaunted Luftwaffe. But the German air force in late November 1942 was stretched thin to the point of impotence. The rising tempo of battle in North Africa demanded the transfer of 400 front-line combat aircraft from the eastern front, reducing effective strength by 30 percent. According to OKW estimates, of 2,000 aircraft of all types in the east, only 1,120 were even operational. Except in a few localized sectors—of which Stalingrad was not one—control of the air began to pass to the Soviets. That is, when the atrocious weather permitted the planes to fly.

Thus the Germans despaired of help from their Luftwaffe when the Soviets released the southern prong of their long-planned and brilliantly executed pincers movement. On November 20, the Soviet Fifty-First and Fifty-Seventh armies under General Andrei Yeremenko, overall chief of the Stalingrad front, plunged into the German salient from the Sarpa Lakes district south of the city. Again, the Rumanians melted away, like snow before a blowtorch. And again, a German armored unit, stationed in reserve, tried to blunt the Soviet attack. The 29th Motorized Infantry Division under General Hans-Georg Leyser charged toward the sounds of gunfire on the morning of November 20, its fifty-five Panzer III and Panzer IV tanks emerg-ing from banks of ground fog to find the Soviet XIII Mechanized Corps dead ahead, ninety tanks, range 400 yards. Instantly, the panzers of the 29th buttoned up their hatches and opened fire. The Soviets were not used to—or good at—surprise engagements. Dozens of T-34s were hit and set ablaze, while others wheeled about in confusion. The artillery battalions of the German division then zeroed in on a railway train that was bringing up Soviet infantry and poured shells into the packed boxcars.

The breakthrough of the Soviet Fifty-Seventh Army had been smashed. The German 29th Division, along with other units of Lieut. General Erwin Jaenecke's IV Corps, wheeled and prepared to slam into the still-advancing Soviet Fifty-First Army. Before they could move, however, an order arrived from Army Group B headquarters, far to the west, to break off any attacks and adopt defensive positions, forming a line to cover the Sixth Army units in and around Stalingrad. With this, the last hope of stopping the Soviet

Ringed by their troops, Soviet brigade commanders embrace after joining forces at Sovetski, about forty miles west of Stalingrad, on November 23. In four days, they encircled twenty German and two Rumanian divisions in a successful pincers movement to reclaim Stalingrad.

attack from the south evaporated. The Russians, of course, were not heading for Stalingrad, but were aiming instead far to the west, to link up with the Soviet forces streaming toward Kalach from the north.

The sky was alight with green recognition flares at 4:00 p.m. on November 23 as the two Soviet pincers met near the town of Sovetski, about twelve miles southeast of Kalach. The great armored trap had clanged shut. Within its jaws was Paulus's entire Sixth Army plus numerous elements of Hoth's Fourth Panzer Army: In all, twenty-two divisions, about 250,000 men, were squeezed into a pocket perhaps thirty miles long and twenty miles wide. It was one of the most extraordinary encirclements in military history, reminiscent of the enormous traps sprung by the Germans during the first months of Operation Barbarossa in 1941 at Kiev and Bryansk. What was more, the creation of the Stalingrad *Kessel*, or Cauldron, as it would be called, marked a shift in the fortunes of war on the eastern front. Henceforth, the German armed forces in the Soviet Union would be primarily on the defensive, fighting more for survival than for victory.

The danger to the Sixth Army had been obvious from the start to Paulus, to General Maximilian von Weichs, head of Army Group B, and to most of their subordinate commanders as well. As early as November 21, when it became apparent that neither the northern nor the southern Soviet pincer could be stopped, Weichs had signaled Hitler's headquarters at Rastenburg in East Prussia, urging that Stalingrad be abandoned and that the Sixth Army retreat 100 miles southwest to new positions on the lower Don and Chir rivers. In response, back came a *Führerbefehl*, the highest-priority Hitler decree, stating: "Sixth Army will hold positions despite threat of

At a frigid Luftwaffe base only fifty minutes by air from their starving colleagues inside the Stalingrad pocket, two German mechanics (above) inspect the elevated plywood boxes they built to shield the wing engines of a Ju 52 supply plane from the harsh cold.

Luftwaffe ground crewmen inch a Ju 52 onto a snowy runway west of the Stalingrad Cauldron. During its desperate airlift to Stalingrad, the Luftwaffe lost 490 transports, including nearly half its fleet of 750 Ju 52s.

temporary encirclement. Special orders regarding air supply will follow."

But the prospect of supplying the trapped armies by air seemed impossible. When Lieut. General Martin Fiebig, the Luftwaffe's supply chief, heard of the scheme, he called his superior, General Wolfram von Richthofen, who in turn phoned Hans Jeschonnek, Luftwaffe chief of staff. "You've got to stop it," raged Richthofen. "In the filthy weather we have here there's not a hope of supplying an army of 250,000 men from the air. It's stark, raving madness!"

At seven o'clock the next evening, from his headquarters at Gumrak in the center of the salient, General Paulus sent an urgent cable to Army Group B for transmittal to the Führer: He was almost out of fuel. Ammunition was growing short. The men had rations for only six days. "Request freedom of action," pleaded Paulus. "Situation might compel abandonment of Stalingrad and northern front." Three hours later, Paulus received a vague reply from Adolf Hitler: "Sixth Army must know that I am doing everything to help and to relieve it. I shall issue my orders in good time."

More exchanges followed as the situation worsened, with Paulus growing ever more urgent in his requests for freedom of action and Hitler becoming increasingly rigid in his demand that the Sixth Army stay put. Then, on the night of November 23, something happened that enraged Hitler and froze his verdict. Paulus's officers had been discussing a retreat among themselves, and one general, Walter von Seydlitz-Kurzbach, commander of the 94th Infantry Division, decided to take matters into his own hands. He calculated that if he started a retreat on his own, the entire army would follow and force Paulus to order a withdrawal from the Cauldron.

The 94th's supply and ammunition dumps were set ablaze, bunkers blown up, and secret documents burned; senior officers removed their distinctive red-striped trousers and donned common garb. Then the division left its positions—and the Russians, alerted by the fires, fell upon them with howling cries of "Urrah! Urrah! Urrah!" Hundreds of soldiers were slaughtered. Seydlitz-Kurzbach's anticipated mass retreat never took place. The other units held their positions. It was a debacle, but the general remained defiantly unrepentant, insisting that his strategy of mass stampede, whatever the losses, was the only correct one. Paulus, incredibly, did not remove him from command.

When the news reached Rastenburg, Hitler flew into a rage. Blaming Paulus for the disobedience, he fired off another *Führerbefehl* at 8:30 a.m.

on November 24th: "Sixth Army will adopt hedgehog defense. Present Volga front and northern front to be held at all costs. Supplies coming by air."

It remains unclear precisely how the airlift decision evolved. By some accounts, Göring personally reassured Hitler at the Rastenburg headquarters, in the face of shouting opposition by the chief of the army high command, General Kurt Zeitzler. "My Führer," the Reich marshal is reported to have said, "I announce that the Luftwaffe will supply the Sixth Army by air." Other accounts have Göring's chief of staff, General Hans Jeschonnek, delivering his boss's promise, but hedging it with conditions about the security of airfields and passable flying weather.

Whatever the case, a successful airlift was manifestly impossible. There were a quarter of a million men to feed, 1,800 guns needing ammunition, 10,000 motor vehicles requiring fuel. Meeting such demands would require a fleet of 1,000 trimotor Junkers 52 transports, each with a load capacity of 2,000 pounds. But only 750 Ju 52s existed in the Luftwaffe's air-transport force, and hundreds of these were spread over Europe and Africa. Moreover, of the seven airfields within the Stalingrad pocket, six were mere airstrips; only one, the main field at Pitomnik, had lights for night operations. Worse, the Red Air Force had concentrated more than 1,000 fighters in the Stalingrad area, making it lethal for lumbering transports. And then there was the weather.

The airlift began on November 25 from two Luftwaffe bomber bases at Tatsinskaya and Morozovsk, west of the Don. In charge was General Fiebig, who watched anxiously as flights of Ju 52s arrived from the far ends of the German empire, loaded up, and thundered aloft. They flew in and out for only two days before a snowstorm shut down the fields. Fiebig calculated that barely 130 tons had been delivered so far—against an absolute minimum requirement of 500 tons each day. "We are trying to fly but it's impossible," he wrote in his diary. "Here at Tatsinskaya one snowstorm succeeds another. Situation desperate."

Slowly the airlift improved, but only a bit. On November 30, Fiebig added 40 Heinkel 111 bombers, each with a capacity of 1,000 pounds, to his fleet. A radio beacon at Pitomnik airfield helped the pilots home in through fog and snow squalls. Ground crews became increasingly efficient. They swiftly drained fuel not needed for return flights and added it to the Sixth Army's dwindling reserves. Returning transports routinely carried out wounded German troops. But Soviet fighters were taking a terrible toll. On November 29, Fiebig sent out 38 Ju 52s and 21 He 111s; only 12 of the Junkers and 13 of the Heinkels made it to the pocket; the next day, 30 Junkers and 36 Heinkels landed out of the 39 and 38 aircraft committed.

By the end of the first week in December, Paulus and his trapped army

New Gear
for Winter
Survival

Even before the end of the German army's first disastrous encounter with the merciless Russian winter in 1941-42, Wehrmacht planners, driven by the picture of German soldiers freezing in threadbare summer uniforms, ordered the development of large stocks of cold-weather clothing. The new designs included a system of garments intended to be worn over the standard wool uniform, and clothing for special duties.

When it became apparent that their soldiers would spend a second winter in Russia, the German army stockpiled cold-weather gear at depots in Poland and the Soviet Union. By the onset of winter, most of the front-line units had received sufficient stocks.

A veteran of the first winter, returning to the front, recalled his troop train stopping to take on winter gear: "Under the weight of these clothes we felt huge and clumsy, not knowing any longer how to tote all our equipment. It was almost too much of a good thing. But in general, our soldiers took a childish pleasure in their padded clothing. Each baggage car soon contained a full platoon of Santa Clauses." Behind his levity lay the grim realization that this odd gear held the key to survival.

Men of the Luftwaffe's flak and field divisions were issued heavy quilted suits and a variety of Russian-inspired fleece-lined hats. Felt and leather boots were distributed throughout the armed forces. Snow-white equipment covers concealed a variety of gear, in this case a field telephone.

The army's basic winter outer-wear came in three weights: single-layer, wool-lined, and quilted. Each version was wind resistant, waterproof, and reversible from camouflage (*left*) to snow-white (*opposite page*). The two sides of the suit repeated pockets, flaps, and drawstrings. The outfit included a reversible helmet cover.

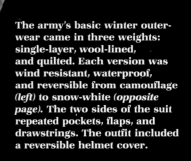

Army regulations decreed that troops fighting in snowy conditions wear colored armbands on their white winter suits to distinguish friend from foe. The winter suit, white or camouflage, was supplemented by heavy quilted mittens and a detachable hood that could be worn under the steel helmet *(above)*.

Small personal stoves provided extra comfort at the front. The Primus-type gasoline stove *(right)* was used for heating food and water, while the shielded kerosene burner *(left)* thawed equipment and provided warmth in dugouts. Antifrostbite ointment *(left front)* was vital in the sub-zero Russian environment.

Drivers, sentries, and other personnel whose duties required them to remain stationary in the deadly Russian cold were prime risks for frostbite and hypothermia. Such men were provided special fleece-lined wool greatcoats, too heavy for active troops, along with massive felt overboots with three-inch-thick insulating wood soles. Some overboots were made entirely of wood and plaited straw.

realized that the airlift was not going to keep them alive. A daily average of only about eighty-five tons had gotten through, less than 20 percent of what was required. On December 8, rations for all troops were reduced to one-third of normal. Men began to collapse from starvation, and a few died, an omen of worse to come.

And still the struggle for Stalingrad continued inside the pocket. On quiet days, snipers on both sides picked off the incautious and dueled among themselves. But there were few quiet days. On the south side of the perimeter one morning, Sergeant Albert Pflüger of the 297th Division waited out a Soviet artillery barrage, then watched three T-34s approach through a smoke screen. Pflüger's 75-mm antitank gun put a shell through the turret of one, blew the top clear off another, and brought the third to a halt with a shell in the undercarriage. More tanks appeared, and Pflüger beat them off with fifteen rounds—only to be upbraided by his incensed commander for expending so much ammunition. To the north, Sergeant Hubert Wirkner and the 44th Division withstood an assault that cost one regiment 500 men, then counterattacked to retake a position that had been held by Austrian troops until they had been overrun. Wirkner found the Austrians lying in the snow, stripped of their clothes; all had been shot.

On the eastern side of the Cauldron, Major Eugen Rettenmaier's existence revolved around three gutted buildings known as the Commissar's House and Houses 78 and 83. The Germans controlled the ruins by day, but the Russians returned to fill the night with exploding grenades, and in the morning bodies littered the stairwells and rooms and cellars. Rettenmaier's men would fight two days just for one room, and most of the Germans who went into these houses never came out. Eventually, the major had to give up House 83, but his troops from the Swabian Alps clung to the others, proud of what Rettenmaier called their pigheadedness.

Stubbornness, raw courage, blind obedience, ultimate faith in the Wehrmacht, adoration of Adolf Hitler—whatever the reason, the morale of the troops trapped in Stalingrad remained amazingly high. In their letters, the censors noted, the men wrote that their Führer would never let them down. "Don't get any false ideas," one soldier wrote home. "The victor can only be Germany." "We are in a difficult position in Stalingrad, but we are not forsaken," said another. "We shall endure." And at the end of November, the men had fresh reason for hope. Word flashed through the beleaguered Sixth Army: "Manstein is coming! Manstein is coming!"

Field Marshal Erich von Manstein was a soldier for soldiers to believe in. Tall, silver-haired, hawknosed, he had been a prime architect of the stunning blitzkrieg through France, had conquered the Crimea and its jewel,

Sevastopol, with equal brilliance, and was one of the few generals Adolf Hitler admired—if it could be said that Hitler admired anyone. Hitler ordered Manstein south from the Leningrad front to command the newly created Army Group Don and mastermind a relief effort at Stalingrad. Manstein immediately conceived a bold plan to send a powerful column slicing through the cordon around the Sixth Army to break the siege. Food, fuel, and ammunition would be rushed through the corridor. Then, with luck—and the Führer's permission—the Sixth Army would break out, escaping through the same corridor. Even before arriving at his new head-quarters at Novocherkassk on November 27, Manstein sent a brisk signal to Paulus. "We will do everything to get you out," promised Manstein, adding that Paulus must hold his fronts and also "make strong forces available soonest possible to blast open supply route to southwest."

Once at Novocherkassk, Manstein ordered a fleet of 800 trucks loaded with 3,000 tons of fuel and other supplies that would follow the tanks into the pocket. A lightning thrust, called Operation Winter Storm, was mapped out from the town of Kotelnikovo along the railroad tracks leading to Stalingrad. Speed was of the utmost importance: It was essential that Army

Panzer IVs of the Fourth Panzer Army assemble with support vehicles on the undulating steppe southwest of Stalingrad shortly before attempting to pierce the Soviet ring around the city on December 12, 1942. The tanks are fitted with track extensions called *Ostketten*, designed to provide better traction in snow and mud.

A Rescue Attempt That Failed

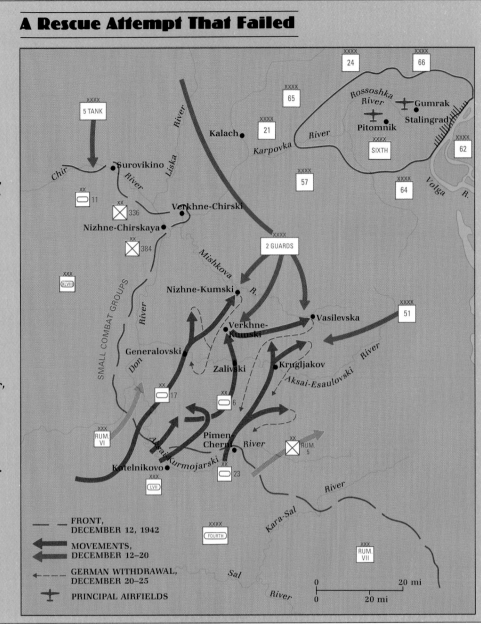

With the Sixth Army surrounded, the Germans pinned their hopes for its survival on an airlift coupled with a relief expedition by the LVII Panzer Corps, composed of two fresh panzer divisions, the 6th and the 23d. The attack, code-named Winter Storm, got under way on December 12 and at first made progress. But once across the Aksai-Esaulovski River, the two divisions bogged down in the gully-ridden terrain against stiffening Russian resistance. After a week of steadily increasing losses, the relief force had only reached the Mishkova River, despite the addition of the 17th Panzer Division. When the threat of another Soviet encirclement arose, the rescuers were forced to turn back, thirty-five miles from their doomed comrades in the pocket.

Group Don strike before the Soviets could tighten their grip on the pocket.

Manstein quickly discovered, however, that his command lacked real fighting power. Its biggest element was the trapped Sixth Army. Otherwise it was, in Manstein's words, "mere remnants." There was a corps-size combat group commanded by Lieut. General Karl Hollidt in place to the northwest, along with elements of the Rumanian army that had escaped attack. But their mission was to guard against another Soviet assault from the north. In the south, General Hoth, with much of his Fourth Panzer Army also trapped in the pocket, could muster only two understrength armored units, the XLVIII and LVII Panzer Corps.

Manstein demanded fresh forces, and the OKW responded by providing him with the cream of the German army. Among the first to arrive, coming up from the south, was the 11th Panzer Division under General Hermann Balck. The general was tough, energetic, imaginative—and ruthless with subordinates. "We were fortunate," he later wrote, "that all commanders whose nerves could not stand the test had been replaced by proven men."

A Commander Born to Serve

Erich von Manstein, Hitler's mainstay in the Russian campaign, was marked for military service at an early age. He was born the tenth child of a Prussian artillery general, Eduard von Lewinski, a member of an old-guard aristocratic family that produced seven generals during the twentieth century. Adopted by a childless aunt, Erich took the name of her husband, Georg von Manstein, whose family tree also held a long line of officers.

Heir to this military tradition, Manstein entered the Royal Prussian Cadet Corps at age twelve, evolving as a bright student and independent thinker with the courage to speak his mind. Severely wounded in World War I, Manstein went on to join the German high command and later to mastermind the blitzkrieg of France in 1940. His troops knew him as a fair and generous commander who preferred to lead from the front. His peers, friend and foe alike, came to regard him as the greatest German strategist of the war.

Two-year-old Manstein, pronounced delicate as a child, is shown with his foster mother and her adopted daughter *(above)*. A model young soldier in the Royal Prussian Cadet Corps *(right)*, he poses with his father, Eduard von Lewinski *(in civilian garb)*, and uniformed uncles. In 1906 Manstein *(opposite, inset, on right)* joined the 3d Guard Infantry Regiment of the imperial army, the same regiment in which his famous uncle, Paul von Hindenburg, had served. Pictured in a 1922 family photo are Manstein, his wife, Jutta-Sibylle, and daughter Gisela.

Balck's division was probably the best on the entire eastern front, and it would soon show its worth.

Racing northward on December 7, the division was approaching State Farm no. 79, fifty miles southwest of the pocket, when it came head to head with a Soviet tank column. The two forces exchanged fire until dusk, at which point the Russians dug in for the night. Not Balck. Leaving his engineers and a few 88-mm guns to mask the enemy, he led his 11th Panzer on a wide arc until, ten hours later, he was astride the route down which the Soviets had come. And there, in the first light of dawn, his men could see a long line of Soviet supply and troop transports driving placidly nose-to-tail south along the road. As he had confidently expected, Balck had found the main body of the Soviet advance that was extending south.

With grim satisfaction, the 11th Panzer swept down alongside the Soviet column, raking the trucks and troops with sheets of machine-gun fire, only twenty yards separating the tanks from their victims. The panzers destroyed the convoy utterly. Balck ordered his gunners not to use their cannon; the time for that would come later. And so it did.

Speeding on south, the 11th Panzer arrived back at the state farm just as the Soviets were engaging the tiny screen Balck had left behind. The enemy tanks spun on their tracks as the panzers attacked from the rear. The battle lasted most of the day, and in the end, fifty-three T-34s were destroyed, while the 11th sustained only minor losses. Balck's division then went on to stamp out a Soviet bridgehead west of the Don and spend the next weeks as a "fire brigade," securing the German center and buying time for Manstein until he could launch his relief force toward Stalingrad.

Meanwhile, another superb armored formation had arrived after a long, arduous journey from France. This was General Erhard Raus's 6th Panzer Division, fully equipped and spoiling for a fight. More units were promised, but Manstein could wait no longer; Hoth was to attack with what he had.

At 5:15 a.m. on December 12, Hoth's LVII Panzer Corps fired up and moved out with 230 tanks, each painted white for camouflage in the snow. Led by Raus's 6th Panzer, the columns headed northeastward toward the southern perimeter of the pocket sixty miles away. Because supply was obviously going to be a problem, each tank carried its own fuel and as much as 200 rounds of ammunition for its cannon.

At first, the German tank crews were mystified by the lack of resistance. In places, the enemy seemed to have disappeared entirely. Greater concerns were the icy terrain and the deep natural ravines called *balkas*, with sides so steep and slippery that even tanks with calks fitted to their treads had difficulty climbing out. It took five hours for engineers to nurse one company of panzers across a particularly bad gully. The division made scarcely twenty miles the first two days. And by December 14, Soviet resistance was stiffening.

Russian troops, hidden in the *balkas*, emerged to harass the German advance, and Soviet reinforcements were pouring down from the northeast. Outside the town of Verkhne-Kumski, forty miles from the Stalingrad pocket, the 6th Panzer suddenly ran into about 400 T-34s, all painted the same ghostly white as their own tanks. Lieutenant Horst Scheibert at first wondered if he had come upon elements of the German 23d Panzer Division, which was moving parallel in support of the 6th. But the gun barrels of the approaching tanks seemed stubbier than those of the Panzer IIIs and IVs. Still, he held his fire. The two formations closed to within 300 yards before the T-34s got off the first shots—and missed. "Fire! Russians!" screamed Scheibert. The two leading T-34s went up in flames, and "the rest," reported Scheibert, "was child's play." Quickly reloading, the German gunners slammed a torrent of shells into the confused Soviets, until pillars of greasy black smoke marked the death of thirty-two enemy tanks.

The tank battles continued for three days before the Soviets finally broke contact and withdrew north. On December 20, with the addition of a third division, the 17th Panzer, German columns fought their way through to the Mishkova River and established a bridgehead on the far side at Vasilevska. The Stalingrad pocket and the waiting Sixth Army were thirty-five miles away. But that was as far as the rescuers could go. By now, the sheer weight of Soviet reinforcements was having its effect, and the vastly outnumbered Germans came to a halt.

The 17th Panzer was down to twenty-three tanks, and its rifle regiment had lost so many officers that it was commanded by a lieutenant. Fuel was scarce, as were food and water. The wounded lay in the snow, some freezing to death in the sub-zero cold. "Our weak troops," one regimental morning report stated flatly, "are insufficient to widen the bridgehead."

The only chance of opening a supply corridor was for Paulus himself to assemble a striking force and drive outward to meet Hoth's tanks on the Mishkova—as Manstein had been urging. But such an effort was fast becoming impossible. By December 19, Paulus had only 100 serviceable tanks in his entire Sixth Army, and Major General Arthur Schmidt, his chief of staff, estimated that there was barely enough fuel for the army to move twenty miles, little more than half the distance to a linkup. "It must also be kept in mind," Schmidt noted in a message to Manstein's headquarters, "that in view of the present physical condition of the men, long marches or major attacks would be extremely difficult."

Schmidt's gloomy appraisal shortly reached Hitler's headquarters at Rastenburg in East Prussia. There General Zeitzler had been beseeching the

Führer to allow Paulus and the Sixth Army to abandon Stalingrad and attempt a breakout. Zeitzler had been so moved by the plight of the trapped men that at mealtimes he had conspicuously begun limiting himself to their reduced rations, losing so much weight after several days of the diet that an annoyed Hitler ordered him to resume normal eating habits. With Schmidt's report on Hitler's desk, however, Zeitzler lost the argument. "Paulus can't break out and you know it," Hitler declared angrily.

Nevertheless, Manstein continued to prod both Paulus and Hitler, arguing that an attempt had to be made, that a breakout was the only way to save even a portion of the Sixth Army. The replies remained negative. Paulus professed helplessness, saying that his men were too worn down and that fuel was too short to attempt any movement. At one point, Manstein flew in his intelligence chief, a major named Eismann, to reason with Paulus and Schmidt at the Gumrak headquarters. But the two generals refused to listen. "Sixth Army will still be in position at Easter," Schmidt said. "All you people have to do is to supply it better."

In that, Paulus's chief of staff was parroting his Führer. Hitler continued to flatly demand that the Sixth Army hold Stalingrad no matter what; to retreat would compromise "the whole meaning of the campaign," he maintained. Thus Hitler and Paulus reinforced each other, killing all hope that the Sixth Army could be saved. Between them, the dictator and the general had created a tragedy that the Sixth Army would act out in scenes of unimaginable anguish.

As the troops in the Stalingrad pocket awaited their fate, another Soviet avalanche thundered down out of the north. And in its path was the

Ranging far ahead of their supply vehicles, Panzer IVs and half-tracks of the 11th Panzer Regiment attack across a field near Verkhne-Kumski, outside the Stalingrad perimeter. The Germans loaded their tanks with extra fuel and more than double the usual amount of ammunition for the assault.

A Russian soldier, his arms frozen at the ready, lies dead at an antitank position battered by the 6th Panzer Division. The Germans faced ever-greater Soviet resistance as they neared Stalingrad, until finally they were forced to give up thirty-five miles short of their goal.

luckless Italian Eighth Army, responsible for holding a sector on the middle Don roughly 200 miles northwest of Stalingrad.

From the start, Stalin and his generals had been amazed and delighted by the swift isolation of the Sixth Army. Now they were launching an even bolder envelopment, a great sweep far to the west aimed at the key road and rail junction of Rostov, near the Sea of Azov. The plan was not only to cut off and annihilate the rest of Army Group Don and Army Group B, but, more importantly, to trap and destroy General Ewald von Kleist's huge Army Group A, which had driven deep into the Caucasus. Success would deliver more than a million Germans into the hands of the Red Army—and possibly win the war at one thrust.

Earmarked for the attack were four Russian armies, 425,476 men and 1,030 tanks. The first of these troops struck from bridgeheads on the Don on December 16 and slammed into the Italians. A few units resisted valiantly, but most of the divisions were shattered almost immediately. Like the Rumanians before them, the Italian troops panicked, small unorganized groups fleeing as fast as they could through the deep snow. Many men, half-starved and despairing, sat down on snowbanks and allowed themselves to freeze to death. The sides of the roads, one Italian survivor

recalled, were dotted with these grotesque, immobile figures, human statuary marbleized with snow and ice. One large contingent of Italians was trapped in a valley with Russians on the high ground all around, firing down with everything they had into the hapless troops below. Some of the Italians committed suicide by rushing at the Soviets; others put their revolvers to their heads.

By the evening of December 23, spearheads of the Soviet XXIV Tank Corps were 150 miles south of their start line and approaching the huge German airfield and supply center at Tatsinskaya, 125 miles west of Stalingrad. Everything going into Stalingrad, and everyone coming out, went through Tatsinskaya and its sister field at Morozovsk. The air base was jammed with Ju 52 transports. And now the Soviets were about to choke off what little support Stalingrad was receiving.

At dawn on December 24, artillery shells began to fall on the Tatsinskaya runways. General Fiebig, in the control tower, watched two Ju 52s explode. Planes started taking off in all directions; a pair of Junkers collided in midfield and burst into flames; others were shorn of wings and tails. Soviet T-34s appeared on the runways as dozens of Junkers struggled into the air, almost scraping the tank turrets. Finally, when a T-34 charged past the tower itself, Fiebig's aide said: "Herr General, it is time to go." But Fiebig stood transfixed for some minutes longer before boarding his own plane and taking off for Rostov. Soon after, the entire field was overrun. Of the 180 planes at Tatsinskaya, 124 made it to safety, but 56 were destroyed.

Erich von Manstein, recognizing the potential for ultimate disaster, had detached his strongest unit, the 6th Panzer Division, from its bridgehead on the Mishkova, and sent it roaring westward to blunt the Soviet drive. This meant the end of the Stalingrad relief effort. The decision was heartbreaking for everyone. As the 6th Panzer wheeled about, an officer stood rigidly erect in the turret of his Panzer IV, faced in the direction of Stalingrad, and snapped off his finest salute. He then turned and sped away. Paulus and his doomed army would remain on every German mind. But the issue was the survival of the armies in the east.

As Manstein coolly evaluated the situation, it was obvious that Tatsinskaya must be retaken. The place was only eighty miles from Rostov, scarcely three days' drive for a daring Soviet tank commander—and that, of course, was what the Russians had in mind. Yet the enemy, for all his five-to-one numerical superiority, had nothing to equal the caliber of Raus's 6th and Balck's 11th panzer divisions.

Driving north in sub-zero weather, the redoubtable Raus had sent an armored detachment swinging in behind the Soviet XXIV Tank Corps even

Hundreds of exhausted infantrymen, troops of the Italian Eighth Army, trudge to the rear alongside their pack animals after being routed by the Russians. The Italian front on the banks of the Don dissolved soon after the Red Army attacked on December 16, imperiling both Manstein's Army Group Don and Kleist's Army Group A.

as the Russians were mopping up at Tatsinskaya. And in the days to follow, the 6th Panzer clamped a steel grip on Soviet lines of communication and supply. Meanwhile, the 11th Panzer and associated units smashed head to head into the Russians. Caught in the panzers' vise, the Soviets had no chance. By December 28, the Soviet XXIV Tank Corps had ceased to exist as a fighting force.

A few days later, a second Soviet tank corps, the XXV, encountered the 6th Panzer on a stream called the Bystraya and was likewise destroyed. In a brutal night battle, the Soviets tried to exploit the sturdier construction of their T-34s by ramming the German Panzer IVs. But the panzers were too nimble, their drivers too skilled, their gunners too accurate. When the

Soviets attempted to retreat, they fell into a deadly ambush by hidden German antitank guns. By daylight, the Germans had knocked out almost all of the Soviets' ninety tanks, at a cost of only twenty-three German machines damaged. And most of these were put back in combat order by the division's repair crews.

These extraordinary battles on Manstein's front relieved the immediate danger to Rostov from the north. But new and worse hazards loomed from another direction as two entire Soviet armies stabbed westward toward Rostov from Kotelnikovo. Here, all Manstein could deploy for the moment was what remained of Hoth's Fourth Panzer Army, reduced by this time to a mere seventy tanks.

As the danger of encirclement grew, Hitler, toward the end of December, finally authorized Kleist and Army Group A to evacuate the Caucasus. But that would be a long process; the group's main armored force, the First Panzer Army, was on the Terek River, 400 miles southeast of Rostov. Somehow Manstein, Hoth, and the other German generals would have to hold Rostov and its sister city of Bataisk, both with key bridges across the lower Don, for several long, desperate weeks while Kleist escaped.

In the event, Russian fatigue turned out to be the Germans' great ally. The Soviet commanders were plagued by troop exhaustion and supply problems. Try as they might, they could not drive their weary, battered units toward Rostov with sufficient speed. It was mid-January before the Soviet advance guards reached the Manych River, east of Rostov, and established a string of bridgeheads from which to launch the final attack to block the German escape route. By then, Manstein had juggled his forces, giving Hoth added striking power: Balck's 11th Panzer had come into the line, along with the 16th Motorized Infantry Division, another first-rate unit commanded by General Count Gerhard von Schwerin-Krosigk, who had been guarding the gap between Kleist's Army Group A and the forces on the Don.

It was Schwerin-Krosigk's 16th Infantry that made the first saving attack, on January 15. Having learned from papers found on a captured Soviet officer that the Russians were planning to cross the Manych at a village called Sporny, Schwerin-Krosigk pressed forward a panzer company and some motorized infantry along the north bank of the river. Within a few hours, these units had punched their way through the Soviets at Sporny, had taken the high ground in their rear, and had attacked the village itself, knocking out a pair of T-34s and four antitank guns. The Germans next captured the Sporny bridge and dashed downriver, along the southern bank, to smash another base the Russians had established at Samodurovka for their drive on Rostov.

That night, a single German battalion under a Lieutenant Klappich dug

The Race to Rostov

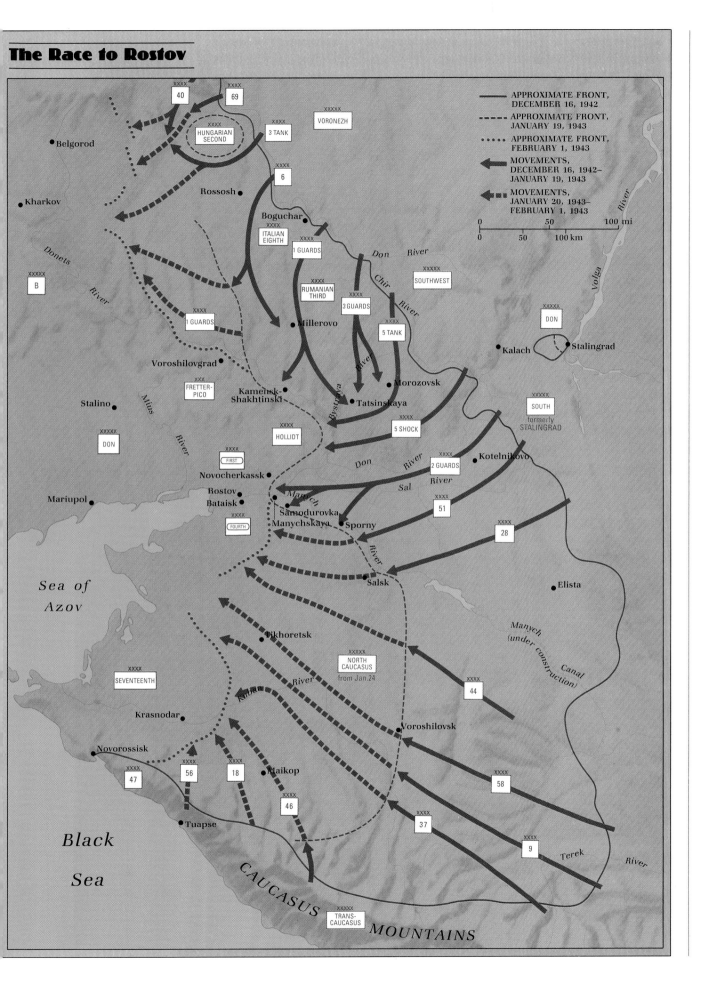

APPROXIMATE FRONT, DECEMBER 16, 1942

APPROXIMATE FRONT, JANUARY 19, 1943

APPROXIMATE FRONT, FEBRUARY 1, 1943

MOVEMENTS, DECEMBER 16, 1942–JANUARY 19, 1943

MOVEMENTS, JANUARY 20, 1943–FEBRUARY 1, 1943

Belgorod

Kharkov

Donets River

B

Stalino

Mariupol

Sea of Azov

Black Sea

Novorossisk

Krasnodar

Tuapse

CAUCASUS MOUNTAINS

XXXX 40

XXXX 69

VORONEZH

HUNGARIAN SECOND

XXXX 3 TANK

XXXX 6

Rossosh

Boguchar

ITALIAN EIGHTH

1 GUARDS

RUMANIAN THIRD

3 GUARDS

Don River

Chir River

SOUTHWEST

Millerovo

5 TANK

DON

Kalach

Stalingrad

Volga River

1 GUARDS

Voroshilovgrad

FRETTER-PICO

Kamensk-Shakhtinski

Tatsinskaya

Morozovsk

HOLLIDT

5 SHOCK

SOUTH formerly STALINGRAD

Don River

Sal River

2 GUARDS

Kotelnikovo

FIRST

Novocherkassk

Rostov

Bataisk

Manych

Samodurovka

Manychskaya

Sporny

River

Salsk

51

28

Elista

FOURTH

SEVENTEENTH

Tikhoretsk

NORTH CAUCASUS from Jan.24

Kuban River

Maikop

56

18

46

47

Manych (under construction) Canal

44

Voroshilovsk

58

37

9

Terek River

TRANS-CAUCASUS

Mitus River

Bystraya

0   50   100 mi
0   50   100 km

131

in at Samodurovka and held the position long enough for Manstein to send General Balck's 11th Panzer to stall the Russian advance. For his part in the action, Klappich earned the Oak Leaves for his Knight's Cross.

Balck and Schwerin-Krosigk now turned to hit the main Russian bridge-head at Manychskaya, where the Manych flowed into the Don, a few miles west of Samodurovka and only about twenty-five miles from Rostov. After duping the Soviets into thinking that they were about to make a frontal attack on the northeastern part of the town, the Germans rolled into the southern part of Manychskaya and took the Russian defenders from the rear. In this fierce little battle, only one German was killed and only fourteen were wounded. Soviet losses included twenty tanks and more than 600 men. Outfoxed by far smaller German forces—by late January the Soviet Second Guards Army had only twenty-nine of its tanks left—the Russians pulled back to reorganize and resupply. The door from the Caucasus remained open at Rostov, and through it poured the columns of the First Panzer Army, which had, in a miraculous month-long retreat, managed to get perhaps 400,000 men out of the Caucasus. The last one, Lieutenant Klaus Kühne, crossed the Rostov bridge on the night of February 7.

There was no hope of similar deliverance at Stalingrad. Christmas Eve had brought a few fleeting hours of cheer for the troops in their foxholes and bunkers. A number of men made small Christmas trees from whatever materials they could find: One tree that adorned a garage next to the Red October steelworks was beautifully carved of wood; others were made of

Using a field telescope to direct their fire *(left)*, Sixth Army troops in Stalingrad aim their 20-mm flak gun at a ground target in January 1943. Having overrun most of Stalingrad in November, the Germans once again found themselves locked in savage street-fighting when waves of fresh Soviet troops *(below)* counterattacked.

scrap metal and decorated with bits of wood, cotton puffs scrounged from medical-aid stations, and stars cut from colored paper. The soldiers gathered around to enjoy delicacies carefully husbanded for the occasion—bits of bread, sips of wine, some cognac, tea with rum in it. In every bunker men sang "O Tannenbaum" and "Silent Night." Then, after dark, thousands of flares vaulted into the sky—green, red, white—like a fireworks display.

The men wrote their wives, children, parents. The messages were full of foreboding as well as expressions of love and faith. "During the past weeks all of us have begun to think about the end of everything," the quartermaster, Karl Binder, confessed to his wife. But Binder was buoyed by a new appreciation of the meaning of Christmas. "It is a feast of love, salvation, and pity on mankind," he continued, that would "tide us over grievous hours." "Nothing can happen to me any longer," Binder concluded. "Today I have made my peace with God."

Christmas Day brought fresh reminders of the reality. The Sixth Army's war diary for December 25 recorded: "Forty-eight hours without food supplies. Food and fuel near their end. The strength of the men is rapidly decreasing because of the biting cold." Bad weather and the attentions of the Red Air Force had cut the airlift to a trickle. Paulus was compelled to reduce rations again: two ounces of bread—a slice the thickness of a man's thumb—and a bowl of watery soup for lunch, and for supper a tin of canned meat when available, otherwise more watery soup. "It is incomprehensible how the men have held so far," wrote Captain Winrich Behr, one of Paulus's aides.

The pressure from the enemy was fast becoming intolerable. A violent blizzard arrived on Christmas Day with fifty-mile-an-hour winds raging across the steppe, and this was followed by a huge barrage by thousands of Katyusha rockets that blasted the German positions, along with shells from mortars and fieldpieces. Then Soviet tanks attacked several points on the German perimeter, most heavily north of Stalingrad in the sector held by the 16th Panzer. Before night fell on the holiest of all Christian holidays, 1,280 German soldiers had died in the Cauldron.

Increasingly, the men realized that they had been abandoned, sacrificed, condemned to die in Stalingrad. "I wish you and the children all the best for the future," Karl Binder wrote to his wife. "Let us hope that we shall be reunited in the other world." Many letter writers were bitter. "It is clear to us that we have fallen victim to gross blunders of leadership," stated one young officer. "If there is a God," another soldier wrote, "He would not permit so great an injustice. I believe in God no longer, for He has betrayed us." There were only two ways out of the trap, still another soldier said with grim humor, "into heaven or toward Siberia."

During the first days of January, forward observers along the German perimeter saw unmistakable signs of a vast enemy buildup. The Soviet high command had decided that the siege had gone on long enough; seven Soviet armies were assigned the task of final reduction. But before launching their offensive, the Russians sent three representatives through the lines under a flag of truce to relay Major General Konstantin Rokossovsky's guarantee that all Germans who surrendered would be treated decently by their captors and given food and safety. Officers would even be permitted to retain their side arms. And all "wounded, sick, or frostbitten" would be given medical treatment.

To make sure that every German soldier knew of the offer and appreciated the consequences of rejecting it, Soviet planes dropped clouds of leaflets, and loudspeakers incessantly blared: "Every seven seconds a German dies in Russia. . . . Every seven seconds . . ." In an especially pointed ploy, field kitchens were set up where the wind would blow the aroma of hot food into the German lines.

Paulus submitted the surrender proposal to Hitler and again requested "freedom of action." The answer came back quickly: The Sixth Army, commanded Hitler, would "fight to the death," and he added, "Every day the army holds out helps the entire front." In response, Paulus issued an order: "Any proposals of negotiations are to be rejected, not to be answered; and parliamentaries are to be repulsed by force of weapons."

The final offensive commenced at 8:02 a.m., January 10, with a cataclysmic bombardment on the southern flank of the bulge in the perimeter's western side. There, in the Karpovka River valley, 7,000 Soviet artillery pieces opened up along a front barely seven miles long. For two hours, the heavy guns flashed and roared, until the German lines cracked open like an eggshell. The foxholes and dugouts of the 29th Motorized Division were obliterated; the survivors staggered away, shell-shocked and hysterical, mouths, noses, and ears bleeding from the tremendous concussions. Masses of T-34 tanks raced through huge gaps, motorized infantry closely following. The German 3d Motorized Division and the remnants of the 29th fought desperately, but were forced to flee before the hundreds of Soviet tanks advancing side by side as if on parade through Red Square.

In the northwest, a fresh offensive developed, and the Austrian 44th Division dissolved in a torrent of fire; in the southwest, the German 376th Division met a similar end. In the north, yet another massive attack punched a gaping hole between the German 76th and 113th divisions, while at Zybenko, on the pocket's southern edge, the 297th Division was broken apart by pounding waves of Russians.

By the end of the day, the remnants of the fractured divisions were

running for the Rossoshka River and Stalingrad itself. Next morning, Sixth Army headquarters radioed Manstein: "Enemy broke through on a wide portion of the front line," adding later, "Resistance of the troops diminishing quickly because of insufficient ammunition, extreme frost, and lack of coverage against heaviest enemy fire."

Many officers were losing their will to lead, and men were starting to desert. Terror overwhelmed the once superbly disciplined troops. On the road east to Pitomnik, a line of trucks was picking its way past a group of wounded when someone shouted that Russian tanks had broken through. The drivers floored their accelerators and smashed, one after another, into the wounded men, rolling them under the wheels and racing on.

By January 13, eight of Paulus's twenty-two divisions had been destroyed as effective fighting units. On January 16, the main airfield at Pitomnik fell, leaving only the headquarters strip at Gumrak capable of handling any substantial tonnage. In any case, the airlift was scarcely functioning. The Luftwaffe had lost almost 500 transports, along with nearly 1,000 airmen, and only about 75 serviceable planes remained. In one last effort, Field Marshal Erhard Milch, Göring's deputy, took over the airlift and managed to collect another 100 Junkers from all over Europe. But it was useless, for everything depended on a smoothly operating ground crew to unload the planes, and Gumrak was a nightmare.

The field was littered with a dozen or more wrecked planes and other debris of defeat, its runways pocked by shell craters and covered with snow. Some planes that landed were not even unloaded. The best chance was to get people out rather than bring supplies in. Gumrak's perimeter

Sprinting between a pair of abandoned German planes, Red Army troops overrun a Luftwaffe air base west of Stalingrad. The Soviet counteroffensive launched on December 16 captured key German airfields and nearly doubled the distance Luftwaffe supply aircraft had to fly to reach the starving Sixth Army, sealing its fate.

was lined with thousands upon thousands of wounded men, carried there in hopes that they might be evacuated. In improvised field hospitals, army doctors labored over dozens of mangled men while hundreds awaited their turn on the ground outside in cold that was twenty degrees below zero.

The army was determined to preserve certain officers—not necessarily generals—with important skills, and a steady stream of these specialists boarded the planes with the wounded. On January 21, Captain Gerhard Meunch, an expert on infantry tactics, was abruptly ordered to leave his men and fly out immediately. No more planes were flying from Gumrak that day, so Meunch made his way to an even smaller strip at Stalingradski, where three Ju 52s managed to land next morning. The transports had scarcely taxied to a stop before hundreds of wounded men stormed the

After the capitulation of the Sixth Army, Major General Alexander Edler von Daniels (*in peaked cap*), commander of the 376th Infantry Division, makes his way past a dead German infantryman. During the last miserable days in the Stalingrad Cauldron, Daniels was one of several generals who, against Hitler's orders, argued for surrender.

planes. Meunch had no chance of getting on board until he showed his special pass to one of the pilots and followed him in through the cockpit hatch. But then it seemed unlikely that the plane would ever get aloft. Fifty or more soldiers had clambered up on the wings, and they were frantically trying to hang on as the Ju 52 began its takeoff. There was nothing for the pilots to do but gun the engines; as the plane gained speed, the clinging bodies were peeled off, and it staggered into the air.

By January 24, the Russians had overrun all the airstrips, including the one at Gumrak, and all German flights in and out of the Cauldron were at an end. One of those left behind at Gumrak was Sergeant Hubert Wirkner,

Soon after his capture on January 31, 1943, Field Marshal Friedrich Paulus, commander of the Sixth Army, walks from a Soviet vehicle ahead of his chief of staff, General Arthur Schmidt. Paulus, whose car flag and 9-mm Beretta pistol *(above)* were confiscated by the Russians, enraged Hitler by surrendering. Hitler swore that, "just like the old commanders who threw themselves on their swords when they saw that their cause was lost," Paulus should have killed himself.

disabled with arm and leg wounds, who watched in disgust as the stronger trampled the weaker in their frenzy to climb aboard the last planes. More hideous still was the scene that Wirkner witnessed across from the airfield at the nearby Gumrak railroad station. Soviet artillery shells had set the building afire; it was burning brightly and consuming in a gigantic funeral pyre the bodies of German dead that had been stacked against its walls to the level of the second-story windows.

As January wore on and the Soviets methodically ground down successive lines of resistance, Paulus made a final attempt to save the lives of his remaining men. On January 22, he radioed Army Group Don with a message for Hitler detailing how futile it was for the Sixth Army to fight on. "The Russians are advancing on a six-kilometer frontage," he advised. "There is no possibility of closing the gap. All provisions are used up. Over 12,000 unattended wounded men in the pocket. What orders am I to issue the troops, who have no ammunition left?"

As before, Hitler turned a deaf ear. "The troops will defend their positions to the last," Hitler replied, adding in his usual florid rhetoric, "The Sixth Army has thus made a historic contribution in the most gigantic war effort in German history."

Under the merciless bombardment, numbers of German officers and men committed suicide. Some officers shot themselves; others asked a trusted sergeant to perform the rite before taking their own lives. Headquarters units and small groups of men blew themselves up with dynamite charges. Hundreds followed the example of Lieut. General Alexander von Hartmann, commander of the 71st Infantry Division, who stood on the railroad embankment south of the Tsaritsa River gorge and blazed away with his carbine at the attacking Russians until he was chopped down by a machine-gun burst.

Paulus did not take either way out—although his Führer obviously expected something of the sort. Early on January 31, Hitler promoted Paulus to field marshal, reasoning that no German field marshal in history had ever been taken prisoner. But to Hitler's wrath, Paulus allowed himself to be captured, a proud trophy for the Soviets. "Paulus," snarled Hitler, "did an about-face on the threshold of immortality."

The general had taken final refuge along with several hundred of his troops in the basement of the ruined Univermag department store in Stalingrad. Around 5:00 a.m. on January 31, some of Paulus's officers emerged from the store and requested contact with a high-ranking Soviet officer. At the same time, a local cease-fire was arranged. In a few hours, a Soviet brigadier general from the Sixty-Fourth Army entered the basement and laid down the terms of Paulus's capitulation. The Soviet officer was

then shown to another room, where he found the newly appointed field marshal haggard and unshaven but wearing full-dress uniform. Paulus was relieved of his pistol and conducted to a staff car, which took him to a farmhouse in the suburb of Beketovka. There he formally surrendered to General Mikhail Shumilov, commander of the Sixty-Fourth Army.

Only one forlorn gesture remained for Friedrich Paulus: The Russians had prepared an elaborate buffet for their unwilling guests, but Paulus refused to eat until he had Shumilov's word that his men would be given food and decent care.

The remaining Germans surrendered in small groups over the next few days. The fighting ended at the Red Barricade ordnance factory in the northern part of town, where 33,000 men of XI Corps under General Karl Strecker battled on until February 2. At 8:40 that morning, Manstein at Army Group Don received a last message from Strecker: "XI Corps has done its duty to the last. Long live the Führer! Long live Germany!"

The German survivors of Stalingrad's Cauldron were not, of course, well

In February, doomed Germans trudge along a Stalingrad street to prison camps in the east. No campaign decoration was awarded the lucky few who made it home. The only German insignia ever to bear the name of the city was the cross *(right)* designed for a unit that was raised in 1943 to commemorate the 44th Infantry Division, which was wiped out at Stalingrad.

treated by their captors. Russian fury at the invaders—and at the way the Germans often treated prisoners—resulted in numerous massacres. Soviet troops simply shot down bunches of Germans as they gave up. In one instance, the Russians poured gasoline into a Stalingrad cellar packed with German wounded and threw in a match. Many thousands perished on forced marches into the hostile Russian interior; still more died in the trains of packed, unheated boxcars taking them to prison camps deep inside the Soviet Union.

An exact accounting of the casualties at Stalingrad is lost to history. But of the Sixth Army's 250,000 men, it appears that about 125,000 died in Stalingrad in the fighting, or from cold, hunger, and disease. Perhaps another 35,000 were flown out to safety. Approximately 90,000 surrendered during the capitulation. Of their number, scarcely 6,000, one man in fifteen, survived captivity to return home after the war.

As for the Russians, their great victory had cost them upwards of 750,000 men dead, wounded, and missing. ✚

Last Days of an Army Abandoned

While Hitler issued bold orders from his cozy retreat in the Bavarian Alps as 1942 drew to a close, the 250,000 German troops encircled at Stalingrad awaited their doom. "Nobody knows what will happen to us, but I think this is the end," wrote a soldier to his bride.

The airlift ordered by Hitler was crippled by foul weather and harassment from Russian fighters. Supplies that got through often proved useless. One shipment brought four tons of mints and pepper; another

Around me everything is collapsing, a whole army is dying, day and night are on fire, and four men busy themselves with daily reports on temperature and cloud ceilings. I don't know much about war. No human being has ever died by my hand. But I know this much: The other side would never show such a lack of understanding for its men. I would have liked to count the stars for another few decades, but nothing will ever come of it now, I suppose.

brought cases of neatly wrapped contraceptives. On return flights, the Ju 52s and He 111s evacuated 34,000 wounded men, but thousands more were left to perish in the parcel of alien land the soldiers knew as *der Kessel*, or the Cauldron. Once the airfields at Pitomnik and Gumrak fell, the Germans had to rely for sustenance on so-called supply bombs, or canisters that were parachuted in.

Bereft of food, fuel, ammunition, and hope, the men penned farewell letters home on toilet paper, maps—anything that could pass for stationery. The army, however, intercepted these deeply personal missives, allegedly for a survey on troop morale. Stunned by the overwhelmingly negative sentiments expressed in them, the Propaganda Ministry ordered the letters destroyed. Yet some of them survived; excerpts from these last letters from Stalingrad accompany the photographs that follow.

Beleaguered Sixth Army troops prepare a makeshift defensive position at Stalingrad in November 1942.

German soldiers rush to unload an He 111 just landed at Gumrak *(inset)*. Not all the transports made it *(above, right)*.

This will be my last letter for a long time, perhaps forever. It is said that tomorrow the last plane will fly out of the pocket. The situation has become untenable. The Russians are within three kilometers of our last airfield, and once this is lost, not a mouse will get out, not to mention me.

Ground personnel shovel out a Ju 52 ambulance plane on a runway near Stalingrad.

Luftwaffe troops carry a wounded comrade through the snow for evacuation.

Right next to me lies a soldier from Breslau who has lost an arm and his nose, and he told me that he wouldn't need any more handkerchiefs. When I asked him what he would do if he had to cry, he answered me, "No one here, you and I included, will have a chance to cry anymore. Soon others will be crying over us."

We marched in here on orders, shoot on orders, starve on orders, die on orders. We could have marched out a long time ago except the grand strategists haven't come to an agreement yet. Soon it will be too late, if it isn't already. One thing is sure, we'll march once again on orders. Probably in the direction originally planned, but without weapons and under a different command.

Infantrymen deliver rations to the trenches under cover of night.

Here I am, still in one piece, with a fairly normal pulse, a dozen cigarettes. Had soup day before yesterday, liberated a canned ham today from a supply canister. Am squatting in a cellar, burning up furniture, twenty-six years old and otherwise no fool, one of those who was mighty keen on getting his bars and yelling "Heil Hitler" with the rest of you; and now it's either die like a dog or off to Siberia.

Here they croak, starve to death, freeze to death—it's nothing but a biological fact like eating and drinking. They drop like flies; nobody cares and nobody buries them. Without arms or legs and without eyes, with bellies torn open, they lie around everywhere. It is a death fit for beasts.

The feet and limbs of some of the 125,000 German soldiers buried at Stalingrad are visible beneath an endless blanket of snow.

In the Path of the Juggernaut

The bombardment began at 9:30 on the cold, clear morning of January 12, 1943. Russian big guns opened up from the east and west sides of the eight-mile-wide corridor the Germans held south of Lake Ladoga, the thumb of land that had sealed off Leningrad from the rest of the Soviet Union since September 1941. For the second time in six months, this site was about to become a major field of battle.

Even as their comrades at Stalingrad, 1,000 miles to the southeast, tightened a death grip on the German Sixth Army, the Red Army forces on the Leningrad front threw all their might against the entrenched divisions of the German Eighteenth Army defending the corridor. The Soviet Sixty-Seventh Army, comprising five divisions and an armored brigade, massed on the west bank of the Neva River. They waited for the 286-gun bombardment to end before charging across the recently frozen ice. Poised on the east side of the corridor were seven divisions and an armored brigade of the Second Shock Army. The plan called for the two Russian armies to break through the sides of the bottleneck, link up, then push south to the Kirov Railway, Leningrad's sundered lifeline.

The Germans on the east bank of the Neva watched nervously as the first wave of enemy infantry, dim and phantomlike in the distance, moved onto the ice shortly before noon. German machine-gun crews waited until the Soviets were 200 yards from shore and then raked them with devastating accuracy. A second wave started across, then a third and a fourth. By now, the advancing Russians had to pick their way past piles of their own dead and detour around craters blasted in the ice by German shells.

By late afternoon, the Soviets had gained a foothold at Maryino, a village in the northern sector of the corridor's west side. The Russian commander wasted no time exploiting the opening: He concentrated three divisions at Maryino and ordered his engineers to improvise a crossing over the treacherous ice so that his tanks and artillery could follow. The Russians advanced north, south, and east across frozen bogs and snow-covered woodlands. The Germans, with the help of four newly deployed Tiger tanks, beat back the southward thrusts, but they could not stop the others.

Two Germans garbed in winter white and armed with submachine guns probe cautiously for Soviet soldiers amid shot-up Russian T-34 tanks near Leningrad in January 1943. That same month, a massive Soviet attack broke the German stranglehold on the city.

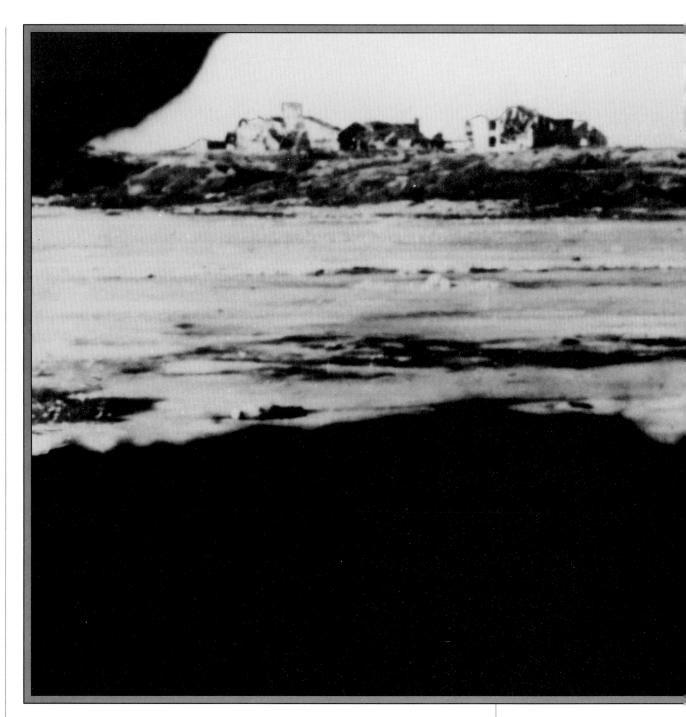

On the eastern edge of the corridor, the Soviet Second Shock Army sent five divisions against a stretch of front only four miles long, punching several holes in the German line. However, a number of strongpoints continued to hold, blocking the way to the vital Sinyavino Hills, which the Russian pincers meant to occupy before driving south to the railroad.

North of this high ground, near the top of the corridor, the Germans were too weak to stem the onslaught for long. By the second day of the attack, parts of two German infantry divisions on the south shore of Lake Ladoga were in danger of being cut off, and the remaining strongpoints to the east had either been overrun already or were fighting for survival. The Russians trapped a battalion of the 207th Security Division near Poselok 8, one of several workers' settlements, each designated by a number, that the Germans had converted into small fortresses.

Photographed from a German gun position, dead Russian soldiers lie scattered across the frozen Neva River east of Leningrad. On January 12, thousands of Soviets were gunned down when they attacked across the featureless ice toward the Germans on the opposite bank.

The 500-man battalion was cut off, and out of radio contact. Trapped, the Germans fought fiercely, pinning down a larger Russian force for two days. On January 15, with ammunition running low, the major commanding the unit summoned his officers and gave them three choices—surrender, hold, or try to break out. The officers chose to break out.

Led by a Russian-speaking soldier dressed in a captured Soviet uniform, the battalion slipped off just before midnight. The hale pulled the infirm across the snow on small, boat-shaped Lapp sleighs, called *akjas*, that they had commandeered from local villagers. Before long, the fleeing Germans spotted a line of enemy tanks silhouetted in the moonlight. Boldly, the Russian-speaking point man approached the Soviet commander, and after a few tense minutes of conversation he returned triumphant: The Russian had taken him for a fellow countryman and had given him the password—

Breaking the Siege of Leningrad

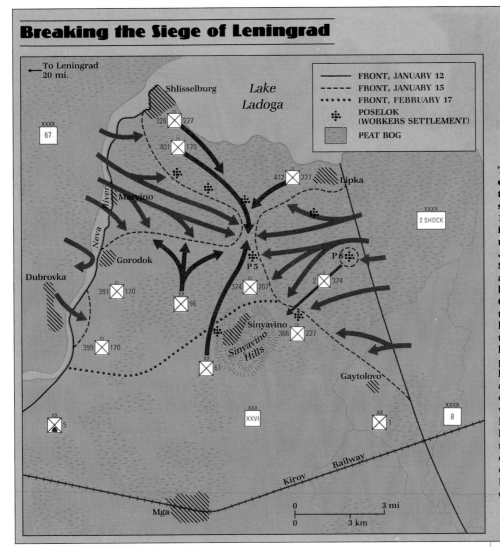

To Leningrad
20 mi.

Shlisselburg

Lake
Ladoga

FRONT, JANUARY 12
FRONT, JANUARY 15
FRONT, FEBRUARY 17
POSELOK (WORKERS SETTLEMENT)
PEAT BOG

Lipka

2 SHOCK

Neva River

Maryino

Gorodok

Dubrovka

P 8
P 5

Sinyavino
Sinyavino Hills

Gaytolovo

XXVI

8

Railway
Kirov

Mga

0   3 mi
0   3 km

The weak link in the German
encirclement of Leningrad was
the eight-mile-wide corridor
south of Lake Ladoga. In August
1942, the Russians tried and
failed to push across it, and then
made a second attempt on
January 12, 1943, when two
Soviet armies hurled themselves
against both sides of the
bottleneck. The divisions of the
German XXVI Corps defending
the corridor inflicted heavy
losses on the attackers, but by
the end of the day the Russians
had broken through at several
points. By January 15, spearheads of the Soviet Sixty-Seventh
and Second Shock armies
converging from east and west
were less than a mile from a
linkup. The Germans managed to
keep them apart long enough for
the units along the south shore
of the lake to escape, but in the
end they could not prevent the
Russians from opening an
overland lifeline to Leningrad.

"pobeda" (victory)—and the location of a gap in the lines. Several hours later, having bluffed past one more outpost and fought their way through another, the Germans reached their own lines.

Gradually the Russians enlarged the beachheads they had forced on both sides of the slender battle zone. The fighting shifted to another workers' settlement, Poselok 5, north of Sinyavino, where the Germans fought desperately to hold open an escape route for units cut off along the shore of the lake. For four days, they held on to this wretched outpost in the middle of a frozen peat bog, and by January 19 the only Germans who had not made it out were dead. In saving themselves, however, the retreating Wehrmacht left behind a land bridge to Leningrad.

The east-west corridor that now joined Leningrad to the rest of the Soviet Union was at most seven miles wide, but it was the city's first land connection in 503 days. Word of their liberation reached the Leningraders by radio at midnight on January 18: "The ring has been burst!" Red flags blossomed in frosted windows, and music blared in the frozen streets.

The Germans had stopped the Red Army's drive short of the Kirov Railway, but Soviet workers immediately began laying track for a twenty-two-mile-long spur through the narrow lifeline. Less than three weeks later, on February 6, the first train rattled safely across, even though the new tracks were within easy range of the German guns at Sinyavino. Unshack-ling the Soviet Union's second largest city had cost the Russians dearly—Red Army casualties in the battles south of Lake Ladoga totaled 270,000 men by the end of February.

Far to the south, a battle unlike any other on the eastern front was un-folding at the German-held city of Novorossisk on the Black Sea. The Soviets here attempted something new and strange to them—an amphibious landing. Even more boldly, they tried to execute it in the dead of night. Inspired by his army's success at Stalingrad, Stalin had propounded the amphibious idea at a Kremlin conference on January 24. Its aim was to cut off General Richard Ruoff's Seventeenth Army by a double encirclement—an attack on the landward side by the Soviet Forty-Seventh Army and a seaborne invasion by marines and commandos, backed by Russia's Black Sea Fleet. The two prongs of the combined operation would link up with other land attacks to the north, blocking Ruoff's line of retreat to the Taman Peninsula, across the Kerch Strait from the Crimea. The amphibious land-

In February, German troops drag sleds loaded with supplies to a new defensive line stretching through the Sinyavino Hills southeast of Leningrad. From this high ground, the Germans could harass trains bringing food and war matériel to the besieged city through its narrow supply corridor. A German colonel declared that if the hills were lost, "the whole siege of Leningrad would be pointless."

After a failed amphibious assault on Germans and Rumanians entrenched around the Black Sea city of Novorossisk, American-made Soviet light tanks and landing craft sit waterlogged and abandoned. Tanks that had been unloaded too far from shore during the February attack spluttered to a halt when water flooded their engines.

ing was the riskiest part of the plan; it was also the most promising because it was the least expected and because the enemy positions on the coast, many of them manned by Rumanians, were relatively weak.

As the Stalingrad drama reached a climax, German reconnaissance units noticed stepped-up Russian activity in the Black Sea and in the port cities of Gelendzhik and Tuapse. Radio traffic also was busier than normal. On February 1, ominously, the jabbering stopped. The German and Rumanian troops on the Crimean coast and the Taman Peninsula—but not at Novorossisk, where a landing was considered unlikely—were placed on alert.

Just after midnight on February 4, an invasion armada moved into position in Ozereyka Bay. The shore was sandy, with scrub grass behind the beach and wooded hills to either side—a perfect landing site. At 1:00 a.m., the first cannonade from the naval guns flashed in the inky blackness. Soviet bombers droned overhead, dropping explosives on the German positions, along with flares to help the navy gunners locate their targets. After an hour of shelling, an assault force of 1,500 marines, augmented by tanks, boarded their landing craft and took off for the beach. They were supposed to be followed before sunrise by a second wave of 8,000 men, consisting of three brigades of marines and a regiment of paratroopers.

As the landing craft approached, Rumanian batteries along the shore and German heavy guns on the high ground opened fire. Searchlights probed from behind the artillery positions, and machine gunners strafed the first marines to hit the beach. Undeterred, the marines knocked out most of the shore positions, and by 3:30 a.m. they had found shelter in the bordering woods. Their commander signaled to the fleet to land the second wave.

But the transports carrying the reinforcements had not yet arrived. It was later discovered that the Soviet fleet command had delayed their arrival on purpose. An interservice conflict had boiled over: The navy preferred to carry out the landing at dawn and had refused to obey orders from the Red Army. Compounding the snafu, the warships that had provided cover for the first wave waited for forty-five minutes, then steamed away. Their orders, it seems, called for them to pull out at 4:15 a.m., and they were adhering strictly to schedule, regardless of the tactical situation.

As the first rays of light streaked the sky, the German gun crews lined up fat targets in the cross hairs of their sights—a fleet of more than 100 unprotected transports, all shapes and sizes, heading toward them. Firing steadily, they set one ship ablaze and sank two more. The admiral responsible for the invasion wavered, unsure what to do. First he ordered the transports, with the troops still on board, to turn to sea and stand by. For one hour, he exchanged frantic signals with the other commands, trying to make up his mind. Finally he ordered the invasion fleet back to base. The marines ashore were on their own. German artillery and infantry drove the stranded Russians back to the beach, where 594 of the original force of 1,500 surrendered. The thirty-one American-made tanks that had come ashore with them were destroyed. Of the remaining marines, 620 were confirmed dead, and the rest either drowned or somehow escaped inland.

But events took an unexpected turn. A smaller detachment of commandos had waded ashore before dawn on the outskirts of Novorossisk. Intended as a diversionary force, the commandos established a beachhead and called in 600 reinforcements. Meeting only scattered resistance, they moved onto high ground behind the town of Stanichka and set up defensive positions. By evening, the diversion had become the main attack.

The Germans mounted a charge that night, but the commandos easily beat them back. General Ruoff now made a major mistake: He waited three days before launching a full-scale counterattack. The delay allowed the Russians to put ashore the original 8,000-man landing force. When the German counterstrike finally came on February 7, the Russians controlled a three-by-four-mile block of land, including the hills behind Stanichka. The invasion that had seemed doomed by interservice rivalry was still alive.

The Russian force that reinforced the commandos eventually numbered 78,500 men. Among them was Leonid Brezhnev, who almost did not survive the campaign. The future Soviet head of state was pulled unconscious from the sea after a fishing boat ferrying him to the beach struck a mine. Although Stalin's amphibious campaign never did trap the Seventeenth Army, the Russians in the Novorossisk area fought on effectively for another seven months, tying down six Axis divisions.

In those first weeks of 1943, the resurgent Red Army seemed to be on the attack everywhere. Five hundred miles north of Ozereyka Bay, in the upper Don region, a powerful force spearheaded by General F. I. Golikov's Voronezh Front completed preparations for an assault on Army Group B, with the main weight of the attack to be against the Hungarian Second Army in the center, south of Voronezh. Golikov had reconnoitered the area for three weeks and moved his troops across the steppe to the attack line after dark to deceive the unsuspecting Hungarians. The objective of this third phase of the great Soviet counteroffensive was for the Voronezh Front, along with the Bryansk and Southwest fronts on its flanks, to thrust westward at three points along a 300-mile stretch and smash the weak northern wing of the Axis forces in the Ukraine. A victory here would open the way for a return to Kharkov and control of the coal and industry of the Donets Basin.

The attack was to begin January 14, but two days earlier a reconnaissance in force drove a deep hole in the Hungarian line, and the offensive was

With readied machine guns, infantrymen from the Second Army hold the German line just outside Voronezh in January. Later that month, the collapse of the Hungarians on the Germans' right flank would force them to abandon the city and fall back westward.

under way. For the first time, the Russians used "mine rollers," metal cylinders pushed ahead of tanks to detonate mines harmlessly and clear minefields quickly. Golikov's troops overran Axis positions all along the line. The Hungarians took the brunt, but the Soviets swept through German and Italian positions on their flanks as well. By January 16, the Axis communication system was shattered; two days later, the northern and southern prongs of the Russian pincers clamped shut around thirteen divisions. After a week, Axis resistance collapsed. The Russians took 86,900 prisoners, along with scores of vehicles and artillery pieces.

Golikov's advance exposed the southern flank of the German Second Army, which was north of the hole left by the Hungarians. On January 28, the Voronezh Front wheeled northward into the rear of the German force, linked up with armor from the Bryansk Front, and cut off two of the German

Operation Star

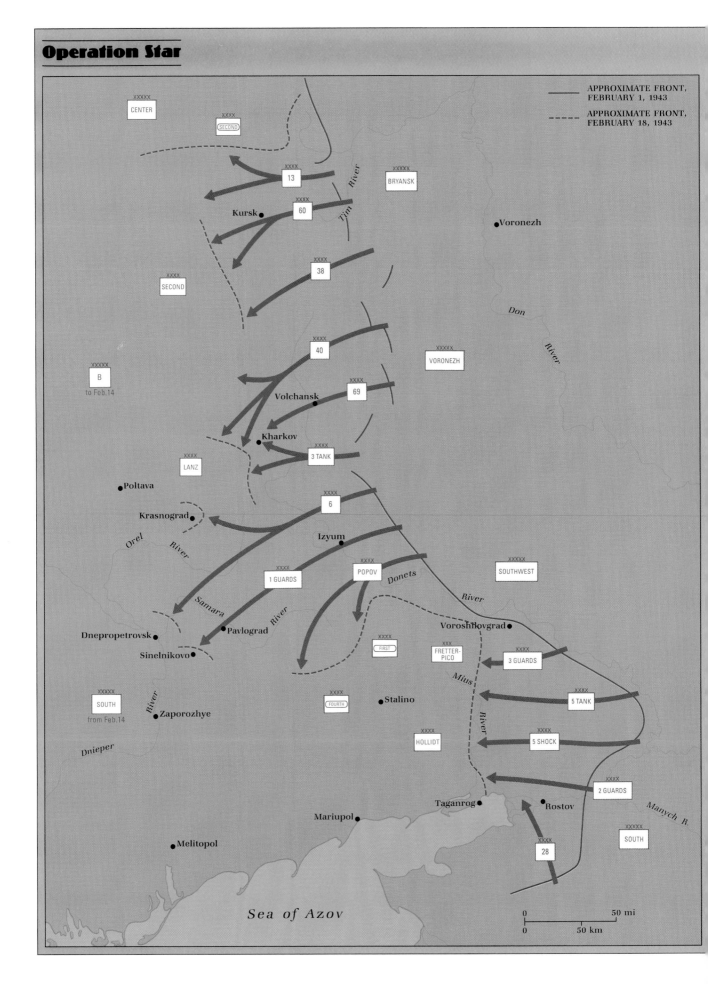

APPROXIMATE FRONT,
FEBRUARY 1, 1943

APPROXIMATE FRONT,
FEBRUARY 18, 1943

CENTER

SECOND

13

60

Kursk

BRYANSK

Voronezh

38

SECOND

40

VORONEZH

Don

River

B
to Feb.14

Volchansk

69

Kharkov

3 TANK

LANZ

Poltava

6

Krasnograd

Izyum

Orel

River

1 GUARDS

POPOV

Donets

SOUTHWEST

Voroshilovgrad

Samara

Pavlograd

River

FIRST

FRETTER-
PICO

3 GUARDS

Dnepropetrovsk

Sinelnikovo

SOUTH
from Feb.14

River

Zaporozhye

FOURTH

Stalino

Mius

River

5 TANK

5 SHOCK

Dnieper

HOLLIDT

2 GUARDS

Taganrog

Rostov

Manych R.

Mariupol

28

SOUTH

Melitopol

Sea of Azov

0   50 mi

0   50 km

164

elieving that the battered German forces behind the Donets ere near collapse, Stalin saw opportunity to crush the emnants of the Wehrmacht in the south and regain the eastern kraine. The first stage of this old plan, code-named Operation ar, was accomplished by the ed of January when the ronezh and Bryansk fronts uted the Hungarian Second rmy and drove the German econd Army back beyond Kursk. hese successes tore a huge ole in the front north of anstein's Army Group Don and ft Kharkov ripe for the taking. uring the first week of ebruary, the Soviets threw a alf-dozen armies into this gap, ree to recapture Kharkov nd the others to turn the northn flank of Army Group Don. espite a dogged defense, harkov fell on February 14. But e even greater danger was to e south, where the Russians ad already turned across e rear of Manstein's army roup and were closing in on e vital Dnieper River crossgs. Hitler could think of othing more than retaking harkov, but Manstein was lready formulating a brilliant lan to save his command and rn the tide of battle.

army's three corps. The German commander, Lieut. General Hans von Salmuth, persuaded Hitler to allow him to evacuate Voronezh. Salmuth's men set fire to the city, then fought their way past the encircling Russians and slogged through the snow and cold to new positions 120 miles west.

The German command now faced a gap in its front nearly 200 miles long, from north of Voronezh halfway to Voroshilovgrad in the south. The situation was perilous. The Wehrmacht had all but exhausted its reserves and was operating close to the bone. By contrast, the Soviets were brimming with confidence. Kharkov was within reach.

At this point, Marshal Georgy Zhukov produced a bold plan to exploit the abundant possibilities. The operation, code-named Star, had two parts: Golikov's force would push west, toward Kharkov and Kursk, while two other Soviet fronts, the South and the Southwest, would drive toward the lower Dnieper and the Sea of Azov. If successful, Operation Star would destroy Hitler's entire southern wing, cutting off both Manstein's Army Group Don and Kleist's Army Group A east of the Dnieper.

The operation began in stages between January 29 and February 2. Stalin hoped to conclude it before the spring thaw. By February 5, three days after the final collapse of the German Sixth Army at Stalingrad, the Soviets were slicing through what was left of the Axis front north of Voroshilovgrad. By now, Weich's Army Group B had virtually ceased to exist. Golikov's right was closing on Kursk; his left and center had reached the Donets River and were preparing to envelop Kharkov. Even more ominous were the spearheads of the Southwest Front heading for the Dnieper River crossings and the rear of Manstein's forces, concentrated in the Donets Basin.

As Manstein read the situation, the first imperative was to pull back his men from the Donets to a defensive line on the Mius River to avoid being outflanked. Hitler, still coveting the coal reserves of the Donets Basin, rejected the request. Manstein persisted, demanding that the Führer reconsider. On February 6, Hitler summoned him to Rastenburg.

Hitler listened with what Manstein later described as "the utmost composure" as the field marshal made his case for a quick withdrawal and consolidation of his forces. Manstein had been through enough of these consultations to know the pattern: The Führer would display an impressive grasp of technical detail, emphasize the importance of will, underestimate Soviet strength, and refuse to yield a yard of Russian soil.

Manstein listened patiently as Hitler embarked on a rambling rebuttal. The field marshal's estimates of what the Russians would do were pure hypothesis, the Führer asserted. He insisted that the Soviets were at the limit of their endurance and that territory should be given up only as a last resort. Hitler concluded with his old economic argument—the importance

165

of retaining the Donets coal—a line of reasoning that enabled him, in Manstein's words, "to display his quite astonishing knowledge of production figures and weapon potentials."

But the field marshal was prepared, and now played his ace. He had consulted with the president of the German coal cartel and learned that the coal mined east of the Mius was of relatively low quality and not important for war production. Hitler was forced to concede the point.

The Führer brought up a final consideration—the weather. An early thaw, he argued, would stop the Russians in their tracks and preclude the need to retreat. But when Manstein replied that he would not stake the fate of German troops on the vagaries of nature, Hitler finally capitulated. The debate had lasted four hours.

During the course of the next two weeks, the Russians made Hitler's hold-the-line argument irrelevant. Nearly a dozen Soviet armies hurtled into the huge breach left by the rout of Army Group B. In the south, a powerful armored group under General M. M. Popov had turned the flank of the First Panzer Army and Army Detachment Hollidt, both of which were

A gun crew from the Grossdeutschland Division loads a 75-mm antitank gun during a battle northeast of Kharkov. In late January, the division hurried from fighting in central Russia to help shore up the shattered German front in the eastern Ukraine.

falling back to the Mius River. In the center, the Russian Sixth and First Guards armies were closing in on the Dnieper crossings, and to the north, the fall of Kharkov appeared imminent. For the few German defenders left in the gap, the fighting had become a series of sharp rearguard actions. These were followed inevitably by retreat, but not before the Germans left a train of destruction in their wake.

The First and Fourth Panzer armies, having escaped across the Don and the Donets, joined Manstein's defensive line, but they were far below strength; companies in the First Panzer mustered between twenty and sixty men. Manstein complained to Hitler that he was outnumbered eight to one. Headquarters told him to expect thirty-seven troop trains per day, but by February 14, only six had arrived.

The task of defending Kharkov, a key crossroads and industrial center, fell to the newly formed II SS Panzer Corps under General Paul Hausser, a sixty-two-year-old regular army veteran who had joined the SS. His corps contained two of the most powerful units in the Wehrmacht, the SS panzergrenadier divisions Leibstandarte Adolf Hitler and Das Reich. Both were fresh from a lengthy stint in occupied France, where they had been fitted with the latest-model tanks and armored vehicles.

In early February, the two divisions, along with several regular army units including the Grossdeutschland Division, fought a series of delaying actions against the onrushing Soviet spearheads. In less than a fortnight, the Germans were driven back toward Kharkov and its outskirts. Golikov's armies were approaching the city from three directions—north, northwest, and southeast—when Hitler declared on February 11 that Kharkov was to be held at all costs, an order passed to Hausser by his superior, General Hubert Lanz. Lanz's command was an ad hoc detachment still technically in Army Group B and not under Manstein's control. Nevertheless, Manstein weighed in with his opinion that the city should be abandoned. The Führer ignored it. On February 13, he repeated his order to hold out.

By now, the Russians were on the outskirts of Kharkov; the ring was about to close. Hausser had already ordered the Leibstandarte to move off to the southwest, leaving Das Reich, supported by the Grossdeutschland, to hold the city. He now requested permission to abandon Kharkov. His corps diary entry for February 14 explains why: "Enemy facing Kharkov's eastern and northeastern front greatly strengthened. All offensive troops tied down in the south. Inside Kharkov, mob firing at troops and vehicles. City, including railway, stores, and ammunition dumps, dynamited at army orders. Systematic withdrawal more improbable each day. Assumptions underlying Kharkov's strategic importance no longer valid. Request renewed Führer decision whether Kharkov to be defended to the last man."

After days of pleading for permission to abandon Kharkov, Lieut. General Paul Hausser, commander of the II SS Panzer Corps, pulled out in violation of the Führer's final order that the city "be defended under all circumstances."

During the German breakout at Kharkov, an SS combat group led by Major Kurt Meyer (foreground) prepares to defend new positions about forty miles south of the city. When the Soviets attacked on the night of February 15 by the light of a burning village, Meyer recalled "firing out of the darkness into the dimly lit rows of Russians."

Lanz was sympathetic but powerless. He told Hausser that the order stood. Late on the afternoon of the 14th, still hoping for command approval of what he had by now decided to do anyway, Hausser signaled Lanz that he was ordering an evacuation that night. Lanz responded immediately: Hold to the death, in accordance with Hitler's order. Hausser phoned Lanz once more, with the same result. He decided to stand fast overnight.

At noon the next day, the Russians renewed the attack. The gap in the Soviet ring was now only a few blocks wide, and Russian guns were shelling the narrow supply route to the west. Just before 1:00 p.m., Hausser, still faithful to the chain of command, sent a final message saying that he was evacuating the city, in defiance of Hitler's order. Late that afternoon, the two German divisions fought their way out of the blazing city to the southwest. If the Führer was incensed at this disobedience, he swallowed his anger when it became apparent that Hausser's withdrawal had saved two veteran divisions and enabled them to link up with other units. Golikov, meanwhile, pushed on west of Kharkov toward Poltava with barely a break in stride.

Stalin, in a message saluting the Red Army's twenty-fifth anniversary on February 22, declared that the "decisive moment" had arrived. Germany was exhausted, he said, while the Soviets were gaining strength. But, lest his soldiers become overconfident, he cautioned that the enemy had suffered defeat but was not yet conquered. Across the Atlantic, President Roosevelt marked the occasion by hailing Russia for "starting the Hitler forces on the road to ultimate defeat."

The Soviet armies rushing headlong for the Dnieper were propelled by the conviction, which came from Stalin himself, that the Germans were making a full-scale retreat. To the Soviet dictator, the abandonment of Kharkov by Hitler's elite troops was proof of a hasty withdrawal. In fact, Manstein was only biding his time. He drew back where he had to but halted well short of the Dnieper, lying in wait, while the overconfident Soviets outran their supply lines.

The units spearheading the Russian advance had orders to continue the offensive "regardless of supplies." Their aim was to reach the Dnieper before the thaw, which normally arrived in late March. But as they pressed on beyond Kharkov, they began to run short of everything that they needed: ammunition, fuel, food. Commanders like Golikov and Popov knew that their supplies were inadequate for an army that might have to stand and fight. And with each mile, their strength diminished.

The German high command was beginning to realize that the best it could hope for on the eastern front was a stalemate. Axis manpower reserves were dwindling; the Führer's forces would have to make do with the numbers

they had, and they were not enough; only by shortening the lines could the Germans effectively deploy their remaining troops. By mid-February, they were giving up hard-won positions all along the extended front.

One of the most difficult sectors to abandon—because it represented a threat to the capital of the Soviet Union—was the salient with its tip at Rzhev, a city on the Volga 112 miles northwest of Moscow. The German troops there had been aimed like a spear at the heart of Russia since October 1941 and had warded off every attempt to dislodge them. To yield Rzhev was probably to yield all hope of capturing Moscow. Yet the disaster at Stalingrad had, at least temporarily, softened the Führer's stand on withdrawals, and in February he ordered the Ninth and Fourth armies in

During the German withdrawal from the Rzhev salient northwest of Moscow in March, German trucks cross the Volga River on a key bridge that has been mined by engineers *(inset)* for ultimate destruction. Hitler considered it so important to blow up the span and thereby hinder the Russian pursuit that he monitored the demolition by telephone from his headquarters in Vinnitsa.

the Rzhev bulge to withdraw 100 miles in order to shorten their front.

The logistics of a retreat of this magnitude were staggering. One hundred and twenty-five miles of roads had to be built, in addition to 400 miles of snow trails for sleighs and horse-drawn vehicles. Two hundred freight trains and truck convoys were needed to evacuate 10,000 tons of matériel. Sixty thousand civilian collaborators and their families had to be moved out. One of the final acts of the withdrawal, code-named Operation Buffalo, would be the removal of 600 miles of German-laid railroad track and 800 miles of telephone line.

The goal was to get everyone and everything out before the thaw. Security was vital: The troops were not told until it was almost time to decamp. But the Russians got wind of the retreat anyway. "Your officers are packing their bags," blared a Soviet loudspeaker on the front line. "Make sure they don't leave you behind."

Sergeant Helmut Pabst, serving in the 129th Infantry Division at Rzhev, kept a journal during the bleak days before and during the great retreat. "We have sat here long enough in the Rzhev bridgehead," he wrote when he learned of the withdrawal. "We are moving out of our dugouts into the snow. Adieu, Rzhev, city of ropemakers and churches. There isn't much left of you."

The freezing wind blew so hard that a man could barely stand erect, yet the Soviets kept the pressure on as Pabst and his comrades prepared to evacuate. On February 17, he wrote that the fighting was "hand-to-hand and knee-to-knee. There was no time to fire, just enough to swing a rifle and club the nearest skull. The enemy left behind three dead and a prisoner."

Pabst's rearguard artillery regiment was among the last to pull out when the full retreat got under way on March 1. Fickle weather made the final preparations a nightmare: The roads were muddy when the withdrawal began, so supplies were packed in wheeled vehicles; when a sudden freeze hit that night, the Germans shifted everything into sleighs.

To Pabst, the terrain they now abandoned was already a no man's land, with, as he described it, "its strange air of excitement and danger in which there are only the vague shapes of fighting men, prowling like foraging wolves. We crossed the Volga bridge for the last time." Hitler himself, anxious to make sure that the bridge was blown after the last Germans crossed, was listening by a special phone hookup when it exploded.

General Walther Model, commanding the Ninth Army, covered his retreat with an elaborate network of mines. In addition to mined roadblocks and conventional antitank and antipersonnel mines, his men rigged diabolically designed explosive devices everywhere an unsuspecting Russian might touch—on doors, windows, inside stoves and handcarts, under stairs, and in temptingly half opened boxes of supplies.

Monitored radio messages attested to their success. "I stable my horse and enter the house," one Soviet commander reported. "There is a big bang, and stable and horse are gone. Those damned Fritzes plant their mines anywhere except where we expect them." The Russian soldiers were ordered not to enter buildings or use wells until mine-clearing crews had carefully combed the area.

Unaccustomed to the painful rigors of a forced march, Pabst and his unit stayed barely ahead of the pursuing Ivans. The wind clawed at his face and tore his uniform. His boots sank in knee-deep snow. "Fatigue gripped my head like a stunning, stupefying cap," he wrote. "Finally it was only my feet that went on marching, step after step, awkwardly stumbling against the wind." The Germans would stop after midnight, only to move on again before dawn. Rising temperatures turned the roads to slush as Pabst neared his unit's new position. A horse hauling supplies, "breathing like a locomotive," twice slid down slippery slopes. On March 14, Pabst reached the new line, with its dugouts, fortified positions, and minefields hurriedly built by engineers and construction troops.

In just over twenty days, the masterfully organized Operation Buffalo had plucked twenty-nine divisions from the 100-mile-long bulge. The new German line before Smolensk was 200 miles shorter, freeing twenty-two divisions to bolster the shaky Axis front, which badly needed reserves.

Sergeant Pabst surveyed his new surroundings, a "miserable tract" of frozen earth enlivened only by the season's first larks. On March 21, Pabst was promoted to lieutenant and placed in charge of an artillery survey section. Six months later, he was killed in action.

One hundred miles northwest of Rzhev, the 100,000 men of the German II Corps, part of Army Group North's Sixteenth Army, faced an even more daunting retreat from their mushroom-shaped salient around the city of Demyansk. Since November, the Russians had tried almost nonstop to slice off the Demyansk salient at its six-mile-wide throat. When the latest offensive, led by Marshal Semyon Timoshenko, subsided in mid-January, the German casualty count had reached 17,767 dead, wounded, or missing, but the salient remained intact. The offensive had cost the Russians 10,000 dead and more than 400 tanks.

Officers on the scene knew that the salient could not hold much longer, and when Hitler on February 1 grudgingly approved the withdrawal of II Corps's twelve divisions over the next seventy days, the army was well ahead of him. For two weeks, staff officers in Demyansk had been carrying out the first stages of withdrawal in secret, and they intended to finish the job a lot faster than Hitler had ordered. The retreat had a code name, Operation Rubbish Clearing, and those who had no need to know otherwise were led to believe that the code referred to a German offensive. Instead, work crews that included Russian prisoners of war began to build snow roads to the rear and lay tracks through the hilly, wooded terrain from the forward tip of the salient to the narrow corridor that crossed the Lovat River. The laborers gave their crude highways such sardonic names as Corduroy Avenue and Silesian Promenade.

Equipment not essential to the front-line troops was extracted first and collected at depots for retrieval later. February blizzards drifted snow over the freshly built tracks through the Valdai Hills, yet in two weeks the army managed to evacuate 8,000 tons of hardware and 6,500 vehicles.

Besides fooling their own countrymen, the Germans staged an elaborate campaign to deceive Russian intelligence. They held noisy "handing-over" parties to salute the arrival of sham replacement units. German radio crackled with bogus messages asking for reinforcements and ordering the construction of facilities for the newcomers. Transmitters beamed signals from the headquarters of nonexistent units.

The Russians may have sniffed out the retreat anyway. On February 15, they unlimbered a new assault from both sides of the Demyansk corridor. They knew that the Germans could expect no help from other eastern front armies, all of which had their hands full. Timoshenko attacked the northern sector of the corridor with six divisions—about 50,000 men; an equally powerful Soviet force hit the line in the south. The German units assigned to cover the withdrawal buckled but did not break. Field Marshal Ernst Busch, commander of the Sixteenth Army, ordered the II Corps to begin a full-scale evacuation without further delay. It would be one of the most daring and dangerous in the history of warfare.

Because of the clandestine head start, German planners estimated that they could extract the corps in twenty days. The men at the forward outposts began their fifty-mile retreat through snow-blanketed hills on the evening of February 17, withdrawing to the first in a series of preselected "interception lines." Every detail had been meticulously planned: Traffic controllers kept the columns moving smoothly, no lights or fires were permitted, noise was kept to a minimum, and repair crews stood ready to respond whenever a vehicle broke down.

The Russian attacks on the corridor sputtered when several divisions were slow reaching the front. As the Germans withdrew, they reinforced their defensive positions at the neck of the salient. By February 19, however,

A German column of horse-drawn wagons pulls out of the Demyansk salient 200 miles south of Leningrad. In February, 100,000 German troops abandoned the peninsula-like projection, destroying whatever they could not transport, including several hundred tons of ammunition and 700 tons of food.

Russian horse cavalry and battalions of ski troops were in full pursuit, harassing the rear guard and slashing repeatedly at the withdrawal route. Another blizzard slowed both pursued and pursuers. During the storm, visibility was so poor that soldiers a few yards apart lost contact with one another; German ski patrols tried to bar infiltrators from the slogging columns; vehicles stalled in three-foot drifts.

Under increasing pressure, the fleeing Germans reached their fifth and sixth interception lines. Heavy fighting flared at the bridges as they passed through the corridor behind the now-gutted city of Demyansk. The Soviets, unable to catch or envelop the retreating troops despite superior numbers, had to be content with the recapture of 1,200 square miles of territory.

Having salvaged every usable weapon and vehicle, the last of the Germans passed out of the Demyansk salient on February 27, just ten days after the withdrawal had begun. A few days later, the weary troops moved north to shore up the forces in the Sinyavino Hills near Lake Ladoga. In the south, meanwhile, the German armies faced an even graver challenge.

Hitler flew into General Manstein's headquarters in Zaporozhye on February 17, still seething over the loss of Kharkov. Only three days earlier, he had awarded Manstein control of all units south of Army Group Center and north of the Crimea, making him commander of a resurrected Army Group South. Now he was prepared to fire the field marshal. But all thought of dismissing Manstein evaporated with reports that Soviet armor was closing in on Zaporozhye. The only senior officer who did get the ax was the expendable General Lanz, who was made the scapegoat for Kharkov.

Manstein briefed Hitler on his overall situation: The line on the Mius River in the Donets Basin was holding, but the strong Soviet forces thrusting southwest of Kharkov toward the Dnieper were already cutting across Army Group South's supply lines. Much of Manstein's new command was threatened with encirclement.

Manstein now presented a daring plan that had been taking shape in his mind. He would concentrate all his mobile formations into five panzer corps—three of which were available immediately—and smash the over-extended Russian columns. General Siegfried Henrici's XL Panzer Corps would take out Popov's armored group while to the north, Hausser's SS divisions would team up with General Otto von Knobelsdorff's XLVIII Panzer Corps to batter the flanks of the Soviet Sixth and First Guards armies. It was a risky proposition, as Manstein would have to weaken the hard-pressed Mius line to muster sufficient forces for the counterattacks. But if it succeeded, the Reich's darkest hour on the eastern front would be transformed into a stunning victory.

Hitler responded by demanding the immediate recapture of Kharkov. Neither man gave way, and their meeting deteriorated into what Manstein called another interminable discussion. They met again the next day and were interrupted by news that ended the debate: The Russians had taken Pavlograd and advanced to within forty miles of the Dnieper and sixty miles of the city where Hitler and his marshal stood bickering. Word came that a third SS division, Totenkopf, earmarked for Hitler's planned attack on Kharkov, was mired in mud near Poltava. Hitler had no choice. He gave Manstein the go-ahead for his version of the counterattack.

The next day, February 19, brought still more alarming news: A Russian armored unit had captured a rail junction forty miles from Zaporozhye, cutting the only rail link to the troops on the Mius. For the moment, no major German force stood between the Führer and the onrushing Soviets. Hours later, the lead Red Army tanks were only six miles from the airfield when Hitler took off in the *Führermaschine*, his private, specially modified FW 200 Condor, escorted by a pair of Me 109s. It was a relieved Manstein who bade him farewell; for a while, at least, he could play his hand without the Führer peering over his shoulder.

On the day Hitler flew back to Rastenburg, the 15th Infantry Division reached the eastern front from France. Its arrival enabled Manstein to try to retake the critical rail junction—at the village of Sinelnikovo—only a day after it fell. The first of the trains carrying the division from La Rochelle, on the Atlantic coast, crossed the Dnieper late on the night of February 19, and Manstein ordered it to keep going to Sinelnikovo—the Germans were going straight into action. The lead train reached the junction before dawn. Three companies of infantry leaped off and overpowered the startled Russians. A second train bearing four more companies, plus antitank guns, arrived in time to help secure the village and beat back a counterattack.

Manstein now gave the green light to the XL Panzer Corps to spring its trap on Popov's armored group, which had just cut the rail line between Stalino and Dnepropetrovsk. While the SS Wiking Division engaged Popov's vanguard, the 7th and 11th Panzer divisions attacked his flanks and rear. By late on the night of February 20, the beleaguered Popov asked his superiors for permission to withdraw. The reply, from General Nikolay Vatutin, commander of the Southwest Front, revealed that the Russian command was still operating on the assumption that the Germans were falling back to the Dnieper. It upbraided Popov for lacking vigor and ordered him not to retreat but to attack.

The three German divisions smashed Popov from all sides, slashing across his supply lines and mauling his fuel-starved tanks and motorized columns. Popov tried to retreat to the north. His superiors, still not grasp-

Field Marshal Erich von Manstein, commander of Army Group South, greets Adolf Hitler at Zaporozhye, Manstein's headquarters 160 miles south of Kharkov. Hitler flew in on February 17 intending to fire Manstein for losing ground, but the field marshal kept his job by presenting plans for a counterattack. Of his disputes with Hitler, Manstein later wrote, "We lived in two worlds."

ing the disaster that was unfolding, signaled him to "use all means available to halt and annihilate the enemy." Instead, it was Popov's army that was being annihilated.

The first thrust in the German pincers movement began on the same day that Hitler made his hasty exit from Manstein's command post. Manstein's order was notably terse: "The Soviet Sixth Army is to be defeated." Hausser's SS Panzer Corps fell hard on the Soviets' northern flank. Stukas from Field Marshal Wolfram von Richthofen's Luftflotte 4 pounded the Russians, and the combined attack routed two Russian rifle corps, opening a gap in the lines twenty-five miles wide.

The other arm of the pincers, Knobelsdorff's XLVIII Panzer Corps, smashed into the Sixth Army's southern flank and rolled on to link up with Das Reich on February 22. The forward elements of the strongest Russian force advancing toward the Dnieper were now cut off from their supply lines and support troops. Soviet Sixth Army headquarters, confounded by

the German turnaround, gave its forward units an impossible command: "Stick to your orders and drive toward Zaporozhye." Meanwhile, the German troops that had destroyed Popov and splintered the leading edge of his army now turned northeast toward Kharkov.

With satisfaction, Manstein read the communiqués documenting the clockwork execution of his risky plan—a last-ditch offensive by an outnumbered and outgunned German army on enemy ground. One dispatch reported that his forces had killed 23,000 Russians and captured 9,000 more. Another reported that Soviet tanks had penetrated to within a few miles of Manstein's headquarters, had run out of fuel, and had been destroyed. Men from the shattered Soviet units were said to be retreating eastward in small bands.

On February 24, the Russian command acknowledged the accuracy of the reports by shifting to a defensive alignment. A makeshift force containing the remnants of several units somehow blocked the advance of the XL Panzer Corps for four days, until February 28, when the panzers finished off Popov's group and broke through to the positions on the Donets that they had abandoned in January. The Soviets tried to relieve the pressure on the Sixth and First Guards armies with a tank attack, but dive bombers from Luftflotte 4 caught the armored units in their assembly area, and the XLVIII Panzer Corps encircled the remnants of the retreating Russians before they could make it back across the Donets.

Manstein was tempted to chase the Soviets across the still-frozen Donets and circle behind Kharkov, but the danger of his troops' becoming stranded by a thaw dissuaded him. By now, the arrival of General Mud was on everyone's mind. The attitudes of the combatants had switched with the

Major Max Wünsche, a battalion commander in Leibstandarte Adolf Hitler, an SS panzergrenadier division, gets his formation moving on the morning of February 21. Two days earlier, Manstein ordered the SS Panzer Corps to attack the overextended flanks of a Russian spearhead that had driven deep into the rear of his army group positioned south of Kharkov.

reversal of their positions: Two weeks ago, the Germans had been praying for an early thaw; now the Soviets were. The Russians had lost 615 tanks, 400 artillery pieces, and 600 antitank guns, along with 100,000 dead and wounded. At a single stroke, Manstein had averted the greatest peril to threaten the Germans since they invaded Russia in June 1941.

General Frido von Senger und Etterlin, whose 17th Panzer Division was part of the XLVIII Panzer Corps, recorded his experiences during the battle in a journal. At one point, his troops spied another column not far off, slogging in the same direction; only after a startled pause did they realize that they were Russians. Another time, he arrived in his armored car to reconnoiter a village at the same moment that an identical enemy vehicle appeared. He also noticed that when Russian infantrymen were overrun, they often played dead—a deception that usually failed. He described the hideous sights that had become commonplace in combat, such as the Russian gunner who had taken a direct hit: "His face hung upside down on his chest," the general wrote, "held there only by shreds of skin."

In little more than a week, the Germans had checked the loss of Sta-

Panzergrenadiers trudge across a snowy field twenty-five miles southwest of Kharkov during mopping-up operations in the last days of February.

The battles in the Ukraine in the first months of 1943 marked the first time that Waffen-SS divisions served together in their own corps. The three SS panzergrenadier divisions of Paul Hausser's SS Panzer Corps—Leibstandarte Adolf Hitler *(the men pictured here)*, Das Reich, and Totenkopf—established their reputations as elite formations during the campaign that shattered the Soviet bid to destroy Army Group South. On his left sleeve, every Waffen-SS member wore a cuff title, an embroidered patch designating his regiment or division *(inset)*. "Der Führer" and "Deutschland" were regiments in Das Reich. The only other German SS unit to serve in southern Russia during this period was the Germania regiment, which fought along-side the volunteers from Scandinavia and the Low Countries in the Wiking Division.

181

lingrad, retained control of much of the Donets Basin, and decimated at least three Russian armies. With the threat of a Russian encirclement gone, Manstein was ready to give Hitler the prize he wanted: the recapture of Kharkov. Fired up by their stunning defeat of the Soviet Sixth Army and parts of two others, the XLVIII Corps and the SS Panzer Corps turned northward toward the city, Hausser on the left, Knobelsdorff on the right. By March 8, their advance units had reached the city's outskirts. The Russians had dug an antitank trench sixteen feet wide and seven feet deep in Hausser's path, but his panzergrenadiers cut steps in its walls and stormed through. By March 11, the Germans had occupied Kharkov's Red Square, although fighting persisted, block by block, house to house, in other parts of the city. Berlin radio prematurely declared the recapture of Kharkov on the night of March 14, to the accompaniment of trumpets and martial music, and the following day a Soviet communiqué conceded

Supporting the attack to retake Kharkov in March, a salvo of rockets from a battery of *Nebelwerfer*, or smoke projectors, streaks toward Soviet positions outside the city. These multibarreled guns, originally designed to lay curtains of smoke or poisonous gas, fired 150-mm or 210-mm rockets with devastating effect.

Manstein's Masterful Counterstroke

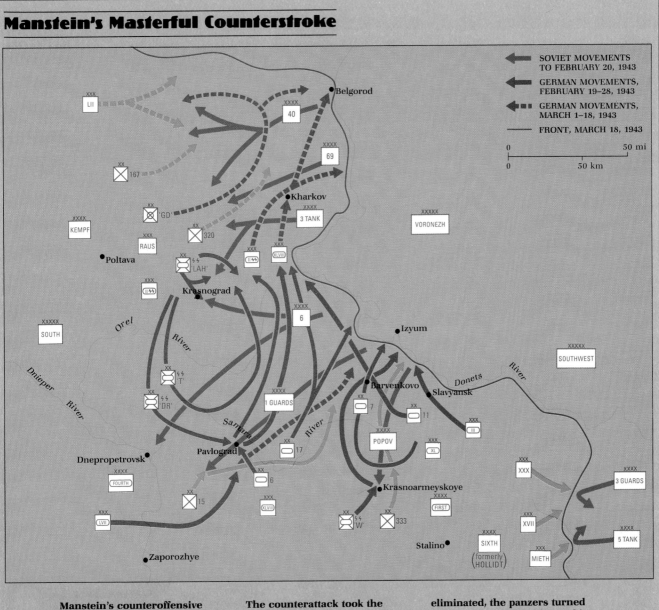

| SOVIET MOVEMENTS TO FEBRUARY 20, 1943 |
| GERMAN MOVEMENTS, FEBRUARY 19–28, 1943 |
| GERMAN MOVEMENTS, MARCH 1–18, 1943 |
| FRONT, MARCH 18, 1943 |

Manstein's counteroffensive began on February 19, when the XL Panzer Corps slammed into the stalled columns of Popov's armored group and the II SS and XLVIII Panzer Corps teamed up against the flanks of the Soviet Sixth and First Guards armies.

The counterattack took the overextended Russians completely by surprise, and by the end of the month the Germans had driven the shattered remnants of three Soviet armies back across the Donets. With the threat to the rear of Army Group South

eliminated, the panzers turned north and succeeded in retaking Kharkov on March 15 after a vicious three-day street battle. After the capture of Belgorod on March 18, the opposing armies finally ground to a halt in the spring mud.

defeat. "Our troops," it read, "after many days of fierce fighting, by order of the command, have evacuated the town of Kharkov."

Three days later the Germans retook Belgorod, a small city north of Kharkov. The Russians fell back behind the Donets to survey the wreckage of their great winter offensive, which had almost achieved glorious success: Fifty-two divisions and brigades, including twenty-five armored units, had been struck from the Soviet order of battle; many that had survived were mere skeletons. Now it was the Soviets who were faced with shattered armies, huge holes in their battlefront, and no ready reserves.

At this point, General Mud made his appearance. The roads and tracks across the broad Ukrainian steppe turned to mush, making troop move-

SS panzergrenadiers, supported by a pair of Panzer IVs, inch their way into northern Kharkov on March 11. After heavy fighting within the city *(inset)*, the Germans succeeded in recapturing Kharkov on March 15.

ments impossible. The war on the eastern front sputtered and stopped.

It was the cruelest of ironies that the positions occupied by the combatants at the moment the thaw halted operations were nearly the same as those the two armies had held a year earlier. Soldiers faced one another across the same ruined landscapes, along the shores of the same muddy rivers, from the same fetid dugouts. All the carnage, the maneuvering, the calculation and high strategy had gained nothing but stalemate—and the prospect of more of the same. Manstein, whose genius had saved the Germans from disaster, had concluded that the best his country could hope for was a draw; that any hope of taking Moscow, Stalingrad, or Leningrad was lost. Yet Manstein's commander, Adolf Hitler, still believed that victory was possible. The Soviets might yet bleed themselves dry, if only the Germans could seize the initiative one more time. ✚

Acknowledgments

The editors thank the following individuals and institutions: England: London—Terry Charman, Paul Kemp, Allan Williams, Mike Willis, Imperial War Museum. France: Paris—Dominique Duperron, Bureau Soviétique d'Information. Germany: Berlin—Heidi Klein, Bildarchiv Preussischer Kulturbesitz; Gabriella Kohler, Jürgen Raible, Archiv für Kunst und Geschichte; Hannes Quaschinsky, ADN-Zentralbild; Wolfgang Streubel, Ullstein Bilderdienst. Dillishausen—Alex Buchner. Freiburg—Florian Berberich, Militärgeschichtliches Forschungsamt. Koblenz—Meinrad Nilges, Bundesarchiv. Munich—Elisabeth Heidt, Süddeutscher Verlag Bilderdienst; Rüdiger von Manstein. Scheessel—Ilse Schmidt-Carell, Paul Schmidt-Carell. United States: District of Columbia—Elizabeth Hill, Jim Trimble, National Archives; Eveline Nave, Library of Congress; George Snowden, Snowden Associates. New Jersey—Al Collett. Virginia—Ray O. Embree, Jr.; George A. Petersen, National Capital Historical Sales.

Picture Credits

Credits from left to right are separated by semicolons, from top to bottom by dashes. Cover: Süddeutscher Verlag Bilderdienst, Munich. 4, 5: Archiv Dr. Paul K. Schmidt-Carell, Scheessel. 6: Bildarchiv Preussischer Kulturbesitz, Berlin. 8, 9: Map by R. R. Donnelley & Sons, Cartographic Services. 11: Larry Sherer, courtesy George A. Petersen. 12: Bildarchiv Preussischer Kulturbesitz, Berlin—Süddeutscher Verlag Bilderdienst, Munich. 14, 15: Ullstein Bilderdienst, Berlin. 16, 17: Archiv für Kunst und Geschichte, Berlin. 18, 19: Map by R. R. Donnelley & Sons, Cartographic Services. 21: Roger-Viollet, Paris. 22, 23: Ullstein Bilderdienst, Berlin. 25: Larry Sherer, courtesy George A. Petersen. 26, 27: Archiv für Kunst und Geschichte, Berlin. 29: Map by R. R. Donnelley & Sons, Cartographic Services. 30, 31: Art by John Batchelor. 32, 33: Archiv Dr. Paul K. Schmidt-Carell, Scheessel—Süddeutscher Verlag Bilderdienst, Munich. 34, 35: Ullstein Bilderdienst, Berlin. 36, 37: Archiv Dr. Paul K. Schmidt-Carell, Scheessel. 38, 39: Süddeutscher Verlag Bilderdienst, Munich. 40, 41: Bundesarchiv, Koblenz, inset map by R. R. Donnelley & Sons, Cartographic Services. 42, 43: Bundesarchiv, Koblenz, insets Ullstein Bilderdienst, Berlin—Bundesarchiv, Koblenz. 44, 45: From *Unternehmen Barbarossa* by Paul Carell, Verlag Ullstein, Frankfurt, 1963, inset map by R. R. Donnelley & Sons, Cartographic Services. 46, 47: Imperial War Museum, London, insets Ullstein Bilderdienst, Berlin (2). 48, 49: Ullstein Bilderdienst, Berlin, insets from *Wir erobern die Krim*, Pfälzische Verlagsanstalt, Neustadt/Weinstrasse, 1943; Roger-Viollet, Paris. 50, 51: Ullstein Bilderdienst, Berlin. 52, 53: Archiv Dr. Paul K. Schmidt-Carell, Scheessel (2); Ullstein Bilderdienst, Berlin. 54, 55: Ullstein Bilderdienst, Berlin, inset from *Wir erobern die Krim*, Pfälzische Verlagsanstalt, Neustadt/Weinstrasse, 1943. 56, 57: Ullstein Bilderdienst, Berlin, inset Larry Sherer, courtesy George A. Petersen. 58: Ullstein Bilderdienst, Berlin. 60: Map by R. R. Donnelley & Sons, Cartographic Services. 62, 63: Ullstein Bilderdienst, Berlin; Alex Buchner, Dillishausen. 64, 65: FPG, New York. 67: Roger-Viollet, Paris. 68, 69: Roger-Viollet, Paris; Alex Buchner, Dillishausen. 72: Archiv für Kunst und Geschichte, Berlin. 73: Roger-Viollet, Paris. 74, 75: Art by John Batchelor. 76, 77: Map by R. R. Donnelley & Sons, Cartographic Services. 78-81: Bundesarchiv, Koblenz. 82, 83: Imperial War Museum, London. 84, 85: Map by R. R. Donnelley & Sons, Cartographic Services, grid from *Stalingrad* by Manfred Kehrig, Deutsche Verlags-Anstalt, Stuttgart, 1974. 88: Georgi Felma, private collection. 89: Bundesarchiv, Koblenz. 90: Archiv für Kunst und Geschichte, Berlin. 91: Süddeutscher Verlag Bilderdienst, Munich. 93: Bildarchiv Preussischer Kulturbesitz, Berlin. 94: From *Unternehmen Barbarossa* by Paul Carell, Verlag Ullstein, Frankfurt, 1963. 95: From *Bildchronik der Heeresgruppe Süd 1941-1945* by W. Haupt and C. Wagener, Podzun-Verlag, Dorheim, 1969. 96, 97: Ullstein Bilderdienst, Berlin. 98, 99: Bundesarchiv, Koblenz—Archiv für Kunst und Geschichte, Berlin; Süddeutscher Verlag Bilderdienst, Munich. 100, 101: Werner Held, Ransbaugh-Baumbach. 102, 103: From *Die grosse Offensive 1942* by Werner Haupt and Horst Scheibert, Podzun-Verlag, Dorheim, 1972 (2)—Süddeutscher Verlag Bilderdienst, Munich. 104: Bundesarchiv, Koblenz. 106: Archiv Dr. Paul K. Schmidt-Carell, Scheessel. 107: Bundesarchiv, Koblenz. 108, 109: Map by R. R. Donnelley & Sons, Cartographic Services. 111: Süddeutscher Verlag Bilderdienst, Munich. 112: Bundesarchiv, Koblenz. 113: Ullstein Bilderdienst, Berlin. 115-118: Larry Sherer, courtesy George A. Petersen. 120: Bundesarchiv, Koblenz. 121: Map by R. R. Donnelley & Sons, Cartographic Services. 122: From *Manstein* by J. Engelmann, Podzun-Pallas-Verlag, Friedberg, 1981—Rüdiger von Manstein, Munich. 123: From *Manstein* by J. Engelmann, Podzun-Pallas-Verlag, Friedberg, 1981; Rüdiger von Manstein, Munich. 126, 127: Bundesarchiv, Koblenz. 128, 129: Fototeca Storica Nazionale, Milan. 130, 131: Map by R. R. Donnelley & Sons, Cartographic Services. 132, 133: Ullstein Bilderdienst, Berlin; Archives Tallandier, Paris. 136: Robert Hunt Library, London. 137: Bettmann Newsphotos, New York. 138: Sovfoto, New York. 139: Soviet Army Museum, Moscow. 140, 141: Imperial War Museum, London—Larry Sherer, courtesy George A. Petersen. 142, 143: Bundesarchiv, Koblenz. 144, 145: Ullstein Bilderdienst, Berlin; J. Piekalkiewicz, Rösrath-Hoffnungsthal. 146, 147: Süddeutscher Verlag Bilderdienst, Munich; © J. Piekalkiewicz, Rösrath-Hoffnungsthal. 148, 149: Ullstein Bilderdienst, Berlin. 150, 151: Bundesarchiv, Koblenz (2). 152, 153: Süddeutscher Verlag Bilderdienst, Munich. 154: Ullstein Bilderdienst, Berlin. 156, 157: Archiv Dr. Paul K. Schmidt-Carell, Scheessel. 158: Map by R. R. Donnelley & Sons, Cartographic Services. 159: Ullstein Bilderdienst, Berlin. 160, 161: Roger-Viollet, Paris. 163: Ullstein Bilderdienst, Berlin. 164, 165: Map by R. R. Donnelley & Sons, Cartographic Services. 166: From *Panzer-Grenadier-Division Grossdeutschland* by Horst Scheibert, Podzun-Verlag, Dorheim, no date. 168, 169: From *Die Leibstandarte im Bild* by Rudolf Lehmann, Munin-Verlag, Osnabrück, 1983; from *Wie ein Fels im Meer: 3. SS Panzerdivision "Totenkopf" im Bild* by Karl Ullrich, Munin-Verlag, Osnabrück, 1984. 170, 171: Archiv Dr. Paul K. Schmidt-Carell, Scheessel. 174, 175: Süddeutscher Verlag Bilderdienst, Munich. 177: Ullstein Bilderdienst, Berlin. 178, 179: From *Wenn alle Brüder schweigen*, Munin-Verlag, Osnabrück, 1973. 180, 181: From *Die Leibstandarte im Bild* by Rudolf Lehmann, Munin-Verlag, Osnabrück, 1983, inset Larry Sherer, courtesy private collection. 182: Bundesarchiv, Koblenz. 183: Map by R. R. Donnelley & Sons, Cartographic Services. 184, 185: From *Die Leibstandarte im Bild* by Rudolf Lehmann, Munin-Verlag, Osnabrück, 1983; from *Wenn alle Brüder schweigen*, Munin-Verlag, Osnabrück, 1973.

Bibliography

Books

Angolia, John R., *For Führer and Fatherland: Military Awards of the Third Reich*. San Jose, Calif.: R. James Bender Publishing, 1985.

Befehl des Gewissens: Charkow Winter 1943. Osnabrück, Ger.: Munin-Verlag, 1976.

Bekker, Cajus, *The Luftwaffe War Diaries*. Transl. by Frank Ziegler. Garden City, N.Y.: Doubleday, 1968.

Bender, Roger James, and Hugh Page Taylor, *Uniforms, Organization and History of the Waffen-SS* (Vol. 2). San Jose, Calif.: R. James Bender Publishing, 1986.

Buchner, Alex, *Sewastopol*. Friedberg, Ger.: Podzun-Pallas-Verlag, 1978.

Burdick, Charles, and Hans-Adolf Jacobsen, eds., *The Halder War Diary 1939-1942*. Novato, Calif.: Presidio Press, 1988.

Carell, Paul:
Hitler Moves East 1941-1943. Transl. by Ewald Osers. Boston: Little, Brown, 1964.
Scorched Earth. Transl. by Ewald Osers. Boston: Little, Brown, 1970.

Clark, Alan, *Barbarossa: The Russian-German Conflict, 1941-45*. New York: Quill, 1985.

Craig, William, *Enemy at the Gates: The Battle for Stalingrad*. New York: E. P. Dutton, 1973.

Degrelle, Leon, *Campaign in Russia: The Waffen SS on the Eastern Front*. Torrance, Calif.: Institute for Historical Review, 1985.

Dibold, Hans, *Doctor at Stalingrad*. Transl. by H. C. Stevens. London: Hutchinson, 1958.

Engelmann, J., *Manstein: Stratege und Truppenführer: Ein Lebensbericht in Bildern*. Friedberg, Ger.: Podzun-Pallas-Verlag, no date.

Erickson, John:
The Road to Berlin. Boulder, Colo.: Westview Press, 1983.
The Road to Stalingrad. Boulder, Colo.: Westview Press, 1984.

Goerlitz, Walter, *Paulus and Stalingrad*. Transl. by R. H. Stevens. New York: Citadel Press, 1963.

Green, William, *The Warplanes of the Third Reich*. Garden City, N.Y.: Doubleday, 1972.

Die Guten Glaubens Waren (Vol. 3). Osnabrück, Ger.: Munin-Verlag, 1977.

Haupt, Werner:
Krim Stalingrad Kaukasus. Friedberg, Ger.: Podzun-Pallas-Verlag, 1977.
Die Schlachten der Heeresgruppe Süd. Friedberg, Ger.: Podzun-Pallas-Verlag, 1985.

Haupt, Werner, and Horst Scheibert, *Die Grosse Offensive 1942: Ziel Stalingrad*. Dorheim, Ger.: Podzun-Verlag, 1972.

Haupt, W., and C. Wagener, *Bildchronik der Heeresgruppe Süd*. Dorheim, Ger.: Podzun-Verlag, 1969.

Held, Werner, *Fighter!* Englewood Cliffs, N.J.: Prentice-Hall, 1979.

Jukes, Geoffrey, *Stalingrad: The Turning Point*. New York: Ballantine Books, 1972.

Kehrig, Manfred, *Stalingrad: Analyse und Dokumentation einer Schlacht*. Stuttgart, Ger.: Deutsche Verlags-Anstalt, 1974.

Kerr, Walter, *The Secret of Stalingrad*. Garden City, N.Y.: Doubleday, 1978.

Kreipe, Werner, et al., *The Fatal Decisions*. Transl. by Constantine Fitzgibbon. New York: Berkley Publishing, 1958.

Kriegstagebuch des Oberkommandos der Wehrmacht:
Vol. 2. Ed. by Andreas Hillgruber. Munich: Bernard & Graefe Verlag, 1982.
Vol. 3. Ed. by Walther Hubatsch. Frankfurt am Main, Ger.: Bernard & Graefe Verlag für Wehrwesen, 1963.

Last Letters from Stalingrad. Transl. by Franz Schneider and Charles Gullans. New York: William Morrow, 1962.

Lehmann, Rudolf:
Die Leibstandarte (Vol. 3). Osnabrück, Ger.: Munin-Verlag, 1982.
Die Leibstandarte im Bild. Osnabrück, Ger.: Munin-Verlag, 1988.

Liddell Hart, B. H., *The German Generals Talk*. New York: Quill, 1979.

Lucas, James, *War on the Eastern Front 1941-1945*. New York: Bonanza Books, 1979.

Mackensen, Eberhard von, *Vom Bug zum Kaukasus*. Neckargemünd, Ger.: Kurt Vowinckel Verlag, 1967.

Madej, W. Victor, ed., *German Army Order of Battle: Field Army and Officer Corps, 1939-1945*. Allentown, Pa.: Game Publishing, 1985.

Manstein, Erich von, *Lost Victories*. Ed. and transl. by Anthony G. Powell. Chicago: Henry Regnery, 1958.

Mellenthin, F. W. von:
German Generals of World War II: As I Saw Them. Norman, Okla.: University of Oklahoma Press, 1977.
Panzer Battles. Transl. by H. Betzler, ed. by L. C. F. Turner. Norman, Okla.: University of Oklahoma Press, 1964.

The Onslaught: The German Drive to Stalingrad. Transl. by Arnold J. Pomerans. London: Sidgwick & Jackson, 1984.

Pabst, Helmut, *The Outermost Frontier*. London: William Kimber, 1957.

Paget, R. T., *Manstein: His Campaigns and His Trial*. London: Collins, 1951.

Philippi, Alfred, and Ferdinand Heim, *Der Feldzug gegen Sowjetrussland*. Stuttgart, Ger.: W. Kohlhammer Verlag, 1962.

Piekalkiewicz, Janusz, *Stalingrad: Anatomie einer Schlacht*. Munich: Südwest Verlag, 1977.

Pitt, Barrie, ed., *The Military History of World War II*. New York: Military Press, 1988.

Plocher, Hermann, *The German Air Force versus Russia, 1942*. New York: Arno Press, 1968.

Reader's Digest Association, *The World at Arms*. London: Reader's Digest Association, 1989.

Salisbury, Harrison E., *The Unknown War*. Garden City, N.Y.: Nelson Doubleday, 1978.

Scheibert, Horst:
Entsatzversuch Stalingrad. Neckargemünd, Ger.: Kurt Vowinckel Verlag, 1968.
Panzer-Grenadier-Division Grossdeutschland. Dorheim, Ger.: Podzun-Verlag, no date.

Seaton, Albert, *The Russo-German War 1941-45*. New York: Praeger Publishers, 1972.

Senger und Etterlin, Frido von, *Neither Fear nor Hope*. Transl. by George Malcolm. Novato, Calif.: Presidio Press, 1989.

Shaw, John, and the Editors of Time-Life Books, *Red Army Resurgent* (World War II series). Alexandria, Va.: Time-Life Books, 1979.

Strassner, Peter, *European Volunteers*. Transl. by David Johnston. Winnipeg, Canada: J. J. Fedorowicz Publishing, 1988.

Tieke, Wilhelm, *Der Kaukasus und das Öl*. Osnabrück, Ger.: Munin-Verlag, 1970.

Turney, Alfred W., *Disaster at Moscow: Von Bock's Campaigns 1941-1942*. Albuquerque, N. Mex.: University of New Mexico Press, 1970.

Ullrich, Karl, *Wie ein Fels im Meer* (Vol. 1). Osnabrück, Ger.: Munin-Verlag, 1985.

Walther, Herbert, *Die 1. SS-Panzer-Division Leibstandarte Adolf Hitler*. Friedberg, Ger.: Podzun-Pallas-Verlag, 1987.

Weidinger, Otto, *Division Das Reich im Bild*. Osnabrück, Ger.: Munin-Verlag, 1987.

Ziemke, Earl F., *Stalingrad to Berlin: The German Defeat in the East*. Washington, D.C.: Office of the Chief of Military History, United States Army, 1968.

Ziemke, Earl F., and Magna E. Bauer, *Moscow to Stalingrad: Decision in the East*. Washington, D.C.: Center of Military History, United States Army, 1987.

Zieser, Benno, *The Road To Stalingrad*. Transl. by Alec Brown. New York: Ballantine Books, 1956.

Index

113, 114, 125, 165, 176
Raus, Erhard: 124, 128
Red Barricade ordnance factory: fighting for, *cover*, 86, 88, 92, 140
Red October steelworks: 132; fighting for, 86, 87, 88, 89, 92
Reichel, Joachim: death and lost orders compromise operation Blau, 24-25, 29, 68
Rettenmaier, Eugen: 119
Richthofen, Wolfram von: airlift for Stalingrad, 112; bombing of Stalingrad, 76; Popov's Sixth Army, attack on, 177; studies defenses of Stalingrad, *94*
Rodenburg, Karl: with Paulus outside Stalingrad, *73*
Rokossovsky, Konstantin: 135
Rommel, Erwin: 8, 25; in retreat after El Alamein, 90
Roosevelt, Franklin D.: 169
Rossosh: 38; Germans capture bridge at, 37
Rossoshka River: 136
Rostov: German objective, 28, 39; Soviet counteroffensive, 127-132; street-fighting in, 61, *62-63*
Royal Prussian Cadet Corps: *122*
Rumanian army: in advance on Stalingrad, 71; with Army Group A, 61; with Army Group South in Crimea, 10, 161; cavalrymen, 66; in Kharkov offensive, 13; morale of, 107; at Stalingrad, 92, 105
Ruoff, Richard: 61, 159, 162
Russian army: active defense strategy, 10; attack on Italian Eighth Army, 126-127, 128; attacks on Army Groups A and Don, December-January 1943, *map* 131; attempt to trap Army Group A in Caucasus, 126-132; casualties on central front, 11; casualties in Crimea, 10, 20, 42, *49*, 56; casualties in Demyansk salient, 172; casualties in Kharkov offensive, 20; casualties at Leningrad, 159; casualties in operation Blau, 39; casualties in Operation Star, 178, 179; casualties at Stalingrad, 84, 88, *127*, 141; casualties in Volchansk salient, 21; casualties in Volkhov pocket, 11; Caucasus, resistance stiffens in, 66; Caucasus, retreat in, 63, 65-66; change in tactics to elude encirclement, 32; counteroffensive against Army Group B, 162-165; disloyalty among ethnic POWs, 67; dogs, use against tanks, 19; interservice conflicts, 161; Kharkov offensive, 13-20; Luftwaffe base overrun near Stalingrad, *136*; minefields, clearing of, 163, 172; Operation Star, 165-169; poor performance in surprise engagements, 110; prisoners lost in Crimea, *53*, 56; prisoners lost in Don envelopment, 71; prisoners lost in Kharkov offensive, *22-23*; prisoners, treatment of, 140-141; propaganda leaflets to German army, 29-32; shift to defensive alignment in Operation Star, 178; stalemate on eastern front, 184; Stalingrad, artillery support at, 87; Stalingrad, counterattacks at, *132-133*; Stalingrad, final reduction of Sixth Army, 135-140; Stalingrad, relief attempt blocked, 125, 126; Stalingrad, snipers at, 87, 105, 119; street-fighting, 61, *88*; troop exhaustion and supply problems, 130, 169; Voronezh, defense of, 34-39; winter (1941) counteroffensive, 7; winter (1942) offensive, end of, 183
Russian army (units): Bryansk Front, 162, 163; cavalry, 174; commandos, 162; Fifth Tank Army, 107, 109; Fifty-First Army, 110; Fifty-Seventh Army, 110; First Guards Army, 167, 174, 178; Fortieth Army, 28; Forty-Seventh Army, 159; militia in defense of Stalingrad, 76; NKVD troops, 61, 83; Second Guards Army, 132; Second Shock Army, 10, 11, 155, 156; Sixth Guards Army, 167, 174, 177-178, 182; Sixty-Fourth Army, 77-78, 79, 139, 140; Sixty-Second Army, 76, 79, 88; Sixty-Seventh Army, 155; ski troops, 174; South Front, 165; Southwest Front, 162, 165, 176; 13th Guards Division, 83; XIII Mechanized Corps, 110; XXV Tank Corps, 129; Twenty-First Army, 107; XXIV Tank Corps, 128-129; Voronezh Front, 162, 163
Russian Army of Liberation: 11, 12
Russian navy: amphibious landing at Novorossisk, 161-162; Black Sea Fleet, 159; interservice conflicts, 161; marines, 84, 159, 161-162
Rynok: German army in, 73-76; Soviet resistance in, 89, 92
Rzhev salient: German evacuation of, *170-171*, 172

S

Salmuth, Hans von: *4-5*, 165
Samodurovka: 130-132
Sapun Heights: 45, 55; German assault on, *52-53*
Sarpa Lakes: 110
Scheibert, Horst: 125
Schmidt, Arthur: 125, 126, *138*
Schmundt, Rudolf: *4-5*
Schweppenburg, Leo Geyr von: 32
Schwerin-Krosigk, Gerhard von: 130, 132
Sea of Azov: 28, 61, 127, 165
Semiluki: 34
Serafimovich: 107
Sevastopol: *map* 40; aircraft and artillery bombardment of, *44-45, 46-47*, 51; British Crimean War cemetery at, 56; fortifications at, 40, 41, *map 45, 50-51*; German assault on, *map 45, 48-49, 52-55*; German capture of, 10, 33
Severnaya Bay: amphibious assault across, 45, 55
Seydlitz-Kurzbach, Walter von: attempted retreat of at Stalingrad, 112-113

Shumilov, Mikhail: 140
Sinelnikovo: 176
Sinyavino Hills: 156, 158, 159; German defensive line at, *159*, 174
Slavyansk: 11, 14
Smolensk: German defensive positions at, 172
Sovetski: encirclement of German Sixth Army completed at, *111*
Soviet air force: bombers, 161; concentrates fighters at Stalingrad, 86, 114, 134; growing numerical superiority of, 93, 110
Soviet Union: civilian casualties in Leningrad, 7; Muslims, anticommunism feelings of, 67; oil production in, 7, 65; spring thaw in, 7, 179, 183-184; supply lines to Allies, 7-8
Spartakovka: Russian resistance in, 76, 89
Speer, Albert: 90
Sporny: 130
SS (Schutzstaffel): *See* Waffen-SS
Stalin, Joseph: amphibious landing at Novorossisk, 159; Caucasus, counteroffensive, 127; concern over loyalty of inhabitants of the Caucasus, 67; Kharkov offensive, 18, 20; Moscow, concern for defense of, 24, 25, 34; and operation Blau, 28; and Operation Star, 165, 169; orders to hold in Caucasus ignored, 63; Sevastopol, orders no surrender in, 56; significance of Stalingrad for, 73
Stalingrad: *map 85*; German offensive plans for, 10, 20, 28, 39, 40-41, 184; terrain at, 83
Stalingrad (advance of German army on): *map* 77; Army Group B orders for capture of, 61; civilian casualties from air raids, 76; combat soldiers in, *91*; Don River, bridgeheads at, 71; Don River, double envelopment at, 71; Dzerzhinski tractor factory, fighting for, 86, 87, 92; fighting in factory district, 84-87, *88*, 89, *102-103*; German vanguard enters, 73-76; Germans tighten pressure on, 78-79; grain elevator, struggle for, 84, *89*; Hill 102, *82-83*; Hoth's advance on, 76-78; Hube's initial assault stalled, 76; Lazur chemical works, 86, 87, 89, *103*; Luftwaffe raids on, 76, 83, 87, 88; Luftwaffe, support of advance, 66, 93; mopping up bypassed strongpoints, 84; near total German control, 89-90; offensive begins slowly, 70-71; panzers, unsuitability in street-fighting, 83-84; psychological significance of city's capture to Hitler, 90; *Rattenkrieg*, 83-84; Red Barricade ordnance factory, *cover*, 86, 88, 92; Red October steelworks, 86-89, 92; Soviet buildup for counteroffensive, 92; Soviet counterattacks on, 76, 86; Soviet troops retreat into city, 78; struggle for ferry landing on Volga, 83, 84; women factory workers in defense of, 73
Stalingrad (Cauldron): air evacuation from, 136-139, 143, *146-147*; airfields at, 114;

airfields overrun by Soviets, *136*, 138; airlift ordered by Hitler, 112, 114, 142; capitulation of Sixth Army, 139-140; Christmas at, 132-134; Commissar's House and Houses 78 and 83, 119; encirclement of German forces, *map* 109; final Soviet attacks on, 135-140, 155; German prisoners at, *140-141*; immobility of Sixth Army, 124-125; letters from German soldiers, 134, *142*, 143, *145*, *147*, *148*, *151*, *152*; Luftwaffe, reduced effective strength of, 110; morale of troops, 119, 134, 136, 142; rations in, 119, 134, *148*; Red Barricade ordnance factory, *cover*, 140; Red October steelworks, 132; relief attempt, *map* 131; relief forces turn back, 128; retreat into by German units, 108-109; Rumanian troops, rout of, 105, 110; Sixth Army and Fourth Panzer Army trapped, 111, 121; Sixth Army war diary report for Christmas day, 134; Soviet buildup, warnings of, 92, 105; Soviet counterattack begins, 105, *106-107*, 108-111; Soviet request to surrender, 135; street-fighting in, *104*, 119, *132-133*; suicides in, 139; trenches at, *142-143*, *148-149*
Stalingradski: airstrip at, 137
Stalino: 176
Stanichka: 162
Stary Oskol: 32
State Farm no. 79: fighting at, 124
Stecker, Karl: 140
Stumme, Georg: 29, 32; compromises security for operation Blau, 24; court-martial of, 25
Sukhumi: German objective, 66, 67, 68, 70

T
Taman Peninsula: 159, 161
Tatar Ditch: Soviet resistance at, 72
Tatsinskaya: fighting at, 129; Luftwaffe base at, 114, 128
Tenning, Otto: 65

Terek River: 66, 70, 130
Thorwald, Heinz: 87
Timoshenko, Semyon: Demyansk salient, offensive against, 172-173; in headquarters at Rossosh, 37; Kharkov offensive, 13, 18, 20
Tim River: 28
Tinguta: 77
Tsaritsa River: 83, 84, 139
Tsaritsyn: 73. *See also* Stalingrad
Tuapse: 161; German objective, 66, 68, 70
Tunisia: Allied landings in, 90

U
Ukraine: German offensive plans, 7; German panzer unit in, *6*; Soviet counteroffensive in, 162
United States: shipment of supplies to Soviet Union, 8
Univermag department store: *90*, 139

V
Valdai Hills: 173
Vasilevska: Stalingrad relief attempt reaches, 125, *126-127*
Vatutin, Nikolay: 107, 176
Verkhne-Kumski: 125
Vlasov, Andrei A.: attempt to relieve Leningrad, 10-11; capture of, 11, *12*; Russian Army of Liberation, commander of, 11, 12
Volchansk: German bridgehead at, 29
Volchansk salient: 13, 21
Volga River: 10, 28, 86, 88, 92; German objective, 71, 73, 76, 77, 79; mined bridges at, *170-171*; struggle for ferry landing in Stalingrad, 83, 84
Volkhov River: 10
Völkischer Beobachter (newspaper): 39
Voronezh: German capture of, 34, *36-37*, 38-39; German objective, 25, 28, 29, 32-34; Soviet counteroffensive, 162, *163*, 165
Voronezh River: 32

Voroshilovgrad: 165

W
Waffen-SS: Das Reich Division, 167, 177, 181; Der Führer Regiment, 181; Deutschland Regiment, 181; embroidered patches of, *180*; Germania Regiment, 181; Leibstandarte Adolf Hitler Division, 59, 167, *178*, *180-181*; II SS Panzer Corps, 167, 168, 174, 177, 181, 182, *184-185*; Totenkopf Division, 176, 181; Wiking Division, 176, 181
Weapons Department: improved tank designs ordered by Hitler, 31
Wehrmacht: *See* Army
Wehrwolf: Hitler's forward headquarters in Ukraine, 59
Weichs, Maximilian von: advance on Stalingrad, 70, 71; assumes command of Army Group B, 39; directed to capture Stalingrad, 61; operation Blau, opening attacks of, 28, 29; operation Blau, planning for, *4-5*; Operation Star, 165; asks permission of Hitler to abandon Stalingrad, 111
Wirkner, Hubert: 119, 138-139
Wolfsschanze: 59; conference at, 7, 8, 25
Wünsche, Max: *178*

Y
Yablenskaya: 14
Yefrosinovka: 28
Yeremenko, Andrei: 110

Z
Zaitsev, Vasily: 87
Zaporozhye: 174, 176, 178
Zeitzler, Kurt: as army chief of staff, 70; opposes Stalingrad airlift decision, 114; recommends withdrawal from Stalingrad, 86, 125-126; replaces Halder as chief of army high command, 70
Zhukov, Georgy: Operation Star, 165
Zieser, Benno: 18
Zybenko: 135

Time-Life Books Inc. offers a wide range of fine recordings, including a *Rock 'n' Roll Era* series. For subscription information, call 1-800-621-7026 or write Time-Life Music, P.O. Box C-32068, Richmond, Virginia 23261-2068.